D1565602

Modern Critical Interpretations

Henry Fielding's
Tom Jones

Modern Critical Interpretations

The Oresteia
Beowulf
The General Prologue to
  The Canterbury Tales
The Pardoner's Tale
The Knight's Tale
The Divine Comedy
Exodus
Genesis
The Gospels
The Iliad
The Book of Job
Volpone
Doctor Faustus
The Revelation of St.
  John the Divine
The Song of Songs
Oedipus Rex
The Aeneid
The Duchess of Malfi
Antony and Cleopatra
As You Like It
Coriolanus
Hamlet
Henry IV, Part I
Henry IV, Part II
Henry V
Julius Caesar
King Lear
Macbeth
Measure for Measure
The Merchant of Venice
A Midsummer Night's
  Dream
Much Ado About
  Nothing
Othello
Richard II
Richard III
The Sonnets
Taming of the Shrew
The Tempest
Twelfth Night
The Winter's Tale
Emma
Mansfield Park
Pride and Prejudice
The Life of Samuel
  Johnson
Moll Flanders
Robinson Crusoe
Tom Jones
The Beggar's Opera
Gray's Elegy
Paradise Lost
The Rape of the Lock
Tristram Shandy
Gulliver's Travels

Evelina
The Marriage of Heaven
  and Hell
Songs of Innocence and
  Experience
Jane Eyre
Wuthering Heights
Don Juan
The Rime of the Ancient
  Mariner
Bleak House
David Copperfield
Hard Times
A Tale of Two Cities
Middlemarch
The Mill on the Floss
Jude the Obscure
The Mayor of
  Casterbridge
The Return of the Native
Tess of the D'Urbervilles
The Odes of Keats
Frankenstein
Vanity Fair
Barchester Towers
The Prelude
The Red Badge of
  Courage
The Scarlet Letter
The Ambassadors
Daisy Miller, The Turn
  of the Screw, and
  Other Tales
The Portrait of a Lady
Billy Budd, Benito Cer-
  eno, Bartleby the Scriv-
  ener, and Other Tales
Moby-Dick
The Tales of Poe
Walden
Adventures of
  Huckleberry Finn
The Life of Frederick
  Douglass
Heart of Darkness
Lord Jim
Nostromo
A Passage to India
Dubliners
A Portrait of the Artist as
  a Young Man
Ulysses
Kim
The Rainbow
Sons and Lovers
Women in Love
1984
Major Barbara

Man and Superman
Pygmalion
St. Joan
The Playboy of the
  Western World
The Importance of Being
  Earnest
Mrs. Dalloway
To the Lighthouse
My Antonia
An American Tragedy
Murder in the Cathedral
The Waste Land
Absalom, Absalom!
Light in August
Sanctuary
The Sound and the Fury
The Great Gatsby
A Farewell to Arms
The Sun Also Rises
Arrowsmith
Lolita
The Iceman Cometh
Long Day's Journey Into
  Night
The Grapes of Wrath
Miss Lonelyhearts
The Glass Menagerie
A Streetcar Named
  Desire
Their Eyes Were
  Watching God
Native Son
Waiting for Godot
Herzog
All My Sons
Death of a Salesman
Gravity's Rainbow
All the King's Men
The Left Hand of
  Darkness
The Brothers Karamazov
Crime and Punishment
Madame Bovary
The Interpretation of
  Dreams
The Castle
The Metamorphosis
The Trial
Man's Fate
The Magic Mountain
Montaigne's Essays
Remembrance of Things
  Past
The Red and the Black
Anna Karenina
War and Peace

These and other titles in preparation

Modern Critical Interpretations

Henry Fielding's
Tom Jones

Edited and with an introduction by
Harold Bloom
Sterling Professor of the Humanities
Yale University

Chelsea House Publishers ◊ *1987*

NEW YORK ◊ NEW HAVEN ◊ PHILADELPHIA

© 1987 by Chelsea House Publishers, a division of Chelsea
House Educational Communications, Inc.,
   95 Madison Avenue, New York, NY 10016
   345 Whitney Avenue, New Haven, CT 06511
   5068B West Chester Pike, Edgemont, PA 19028

Introduction © 1987 by Harold Bloom

Printed and bound in the United States of America

10 9 8 7 6 5 4 3 2 1

∞ The paper used in this publication meets the minimum
requirements of the American National Standard for Permanence
of Paper for Printed Library Materials, Z39.48–1984.

Library of Congress Cataloging-in-Publication Data
Henry Fielding's Tom Jones.
   (Modern critical interpretations)
   Bibliography: p.
   Includes index.
   Summary: A collection of critical essays on Fielding's novel
"Tom Jones" arranged in chronological order of publication.
   1. Fielding, Henry, 1707–1754. History of Tom Jones.
[1. Fielding, Henry, 1707–1754. History of Tom
Jones.   2. English literature—History and
criticism]   I. Bloom, Harold.   II. Series.
PR3454.H7H46   1987   823'.5   87–5831
ISBN 0–87754–949–4 (alk. paper)

Contents

Editor's Note

This book brings together a representative selection of the most useful modern criticism devoted to Henry Fielding's major novel, *The History of Tom Jones, A Foundling*. The critical essays are reprinted here in the chronological order of their original publication. I am grateful to Christina Büchmann for her aid in editing this volume.

My introduction first considers Dr. Johnson's negative view of *Tom Jones*, and then examines the most remarkable figure in the novel, Squire Western. The chronological sequence of criticism begins with Ian Watt's important discussion of *Tom Jones* as a crucial book in the rise of the novel as a dominant form. Fielding's own role as narrator is analyzed by Wayne C. Booth, who salutes this "Fielding" as a created self, comparable to that created work, *Tom Jones*. Martin Price follows with his subtle discussion of Fielding's "saving skepticism" in his play against forms.

Lucianic satire in Fielding is examined by Ronald Paulson, as a context for Fielding's transformation of irony into an investigation of the complexities of reality. The argument of *Tom Jones* is seen by Martin C. Battestin as implicit in the coherence of its form, testifying to Fielding's normative Christian faith in God's providence. Grete Ek treats the London sequence of the novel as a theatrical masque, while Manuel Schonhorn centers upon the gypsy episode that takes place when Tom and Partridge are lost together in the woods.

In this book's final essay, Leopold Damrosch, Jr. reads the novel as a long farewell to Puritan narrative, with its powerful attempt to identify literary form and theological principle. By emphasizing Fielding's deep sympathy with the Puritan vision of God's providence, Damrosch exposes the dialectical element in Fielding's formal inventiveness as a modern novelist.

Introduction

Martin Price remarks that "Fielding can reward his heroes because they do not seek a reward." As a critical observation, this is in Fielding's own spirit, and tells us again what kind of novel Fielding invented, a comic *Odyssey*, ancestor of Smollett and Dickens, and of Joyce's *Ulysses*. My teacher Frederick W. Hilles liked to compare *Tom Jones* to *Ulysses*, while acknowledging that Fielding the narrator was neither invisible nor indifferent. Certainly Fielding was a fabulous artificer, which must be why he provoked so formidable a critical enemy as Dr. Samuel Johnson, who loved Alexander Pope while despising the most Popean of all novelists. Johnson vastly preferred Samuel Richardson to Fielding, a preference I myself share, though without prejudice to Fielding, since Richardson's *Clarissa* seems to me still the strongest novel in the language, surpassing even Austen's *Emma*, Eliot's *Middlemarch*, and James's *Portrait of a Lady*, all of them its descendants. *Tom Jones* founds another line, the rival tradition that includes Dickens and Joyce, novelists as exuberant as Fielding, and metaphysically and psychologically more problematic.

Samuel Johnson evidently resented what he took to be Fielding's simplistic vision, a resentment understandable in a great moralist who believed that human life was everywhere a condition in which much was to be endured, and little to be enjoyed. No one can match Johnson as a compelling moralist, but he necessarily undervalued Fielding's moral shrewdness. The true issue between Richardson and Fielding was in modes of representation, in their different views of mimesis. It is as though Richardson and Fielding split Shakespeare between them, with Richardson absorbing the Shakespearean power to portray inwardness, and Fielding inheriting Shakespeare's uncanny ease in depicting a romance world that becomes more real than reality.

Johnson told the protesting Boswell that "there is more knowledge of the heart in one letter of Richardson's, than in all *Tom Jones*." To Johnson, the personages in Fielding were "characters of manners," but in Richardson they were "characters of nature." This distinction is at least critical; one feels that many modern scholars who prefer Fielding to Richardson do so upon Coleridge's affective premises: "and how charming, how wholesome, Fielding always is! To take him up after Richardson is like emerging from a sick-room heated by stoves into an open lawn on a breezy day in May." That has the same persuasiveness as Richardson's explanation of why he would not read *Tom Jones*: "I was told, that it was a rambling Collection of Waking Dreams, in which Probability was not observed."

The seven volumes of *Clarissa* were published throughout the year from December 1747 through December 1748; *Tom Jones* came out in February 1749. Rivalry between the two novels was inevitable, and both seem to have sold very well. Between them, they established the modern novel, still the dominant literary form after two and a half centuries. Ian Watt, the definitive chronicler of *The Rise of the Novel* (1957), probably achieved the most balanced judgment on Fielding's crucial strengths and limitations:

> In his effort to infuse the new genre with something of the Shakespearean virtues Fielding departed too far from formal realism to initiate a viable tradition, but his work serves as a perpetual reminder that if the new genre was to challenge older literary forms it had to find a way of conveying not only a convincing impression but a wise assessment of life, an assessment that could only come from taking a much wider view than Defoe or Richardson of the affairs of mankind.

II

What is Shakespearean about *Tom Jones*? The violent, daemonic, mindless energy of Squire Western, or the bodily ego rampant, is certainly part of the answer. Martin Price calls Western the finest English comic character after Falstaff, and the judgment seems indisputable. Yet here also a shadow falls. Falstaff, like his precursor, the Wife of Bath, is a heroic vitalist, raising vitalism, as she does, to the sublime of wit. Like Falstaff, the Wife is a great parodist, and a dangerously sophisticated Bible interpreter, as Talbot Donaldson demonstrates. But Western is energy without mind, and so is himself a living parody of vitalism. Fielding's genius nevertheless is so incarnated in Western that he breaks the limits of representation, and leaps out of the novel into that supermimetic domain where Falstaff and the Wife of Bath join Don Quixote and Sancho Panza. Western's simplicity is so exuberant and physical that it achieves a new kind of complexity, as in this astonishing comic reversal:

> *Western* had been long impatient for the Event of this Conference, and was just now arrived at the Door to listen; when having heard the last Sentiments of his Daughter's Heart, he lost all Temper, and bursting open the Door in a Rage, cried out.—"It is a Lie. It is a d—n'd Lie. It is all owing to that d—d'd Rascal *Juones*; and if she could get at un, she'd ha un any Hour of the Day." Here *Allworthy* interposed, and addressing himself to the Squire with some Anger in his Look, he said, "Mr. *Western,* you have not kept your Word with me. You promised to abstain from all Violence."—"Why so I did," cries *Western,* "as long as it was possible; but to hear a Wench telling such confounded Lies.—Zounds! Doth she think if she can make Vools of other Volk, she can make one of me?—No, no, I know her better than thee dost." "I am sorry to tell you, Sir," answered *Allworthy,* "it doth not appear by your Behaviour to this young Lady, that you know her at all. I ask Pardon for what I say; but I think our Intimacy, your own Desires, and the Occasion justify me. She is your Daughter, Mr. *Western,* and I think she doth Honour to your Name. If I was capable of Envy, I should sooner envy you on this Account, than any other Man whatever."—"Odrabbit it," cries the Squire, "I wish she was thine with all my Heart—wouldst soon be glad to be rid of the Trouble o' her."—"Indeed, my good Friend," answered *Allworthy,* "you yourself are the Cause of all the Trouble you complain of. Place that Confidence in the young Lady which she so well deserves, and I am certain you will be the happiest Father on Earth."—"I Confidence in her!" cries the Squire.—"S'blood! what Confidence can I place in her, when she won't do as I wou'd ha her? Let her gi but her Consent to marry as I would ha her, and I'll place as much Confidence in her as wouldst ha me."—"You have no Right, Neighbour," answered *Allworthy,* "to insist on any such Consent. A negative Voice your Daughter

allows you, and God and Nature have thought proper to allow you no more." "A negative Voice?" cries the Squire—"Ay! ay! I'll shew you what a negative Voice I ha.——Go along, go into your Chamber, go, you Stubborn."—"Indeed, Mr. *Western*," said *Allworthy*,—"Indeed, you use her cruelly—I cannot bear to see this—You shall, you must behave to her in a kinder Manner. She deserves the best of Treatment." "Yes, yes," said the Squire, "I know what she deserves: Now she's gone, I'll shew you what she deserves——See here, Sir, here is a Letter from my Cousin, my Lady *Bellaston,* in which she is so kind to gi me to understand, that the Fellow is got out of Prison again; and here she advises me to take all the Care I can o' the Wench. Odzookers! Neighbour *Allworthy,* you don't know what it is to govern a Daughter."

The Squire ended his Speech with some Compliments to his own Sagacity; and then *Allworthy,* after a formal Preface, acquainted him with the whole Discovery which he had made concerning *Jones,* with his Anger to *Blifil,* and with every Particular which hath been disclosed to the Reader in the preceding Chapters.

Men over-violent in their Dispositions, are, for the most Part, as changeable in them. No sooner then was *Western* informed of Mr. *Allworthy*'s Intention to make *Jones* his Heir, than he joined heartily with the Uncle in every Commendation of the Nephew, and became as eager for her Marriage with *Jones,* as he had before been to couple her to *Blifil.*

Here Mr. *Allworthy* was again forced to interpose, and to relate what had passed between him and *Sophia,* at which he testified great Surprize.

The Squire was silent a Moment, and looked wild with Astonishment at this Account——At last he cried out, "Why what can be the Meaning of this, Neighbour *Allworthy*? Vond o un she was, that I'll be sworn to.—Odzookers! I have hit o't. As sure as a Gun I have hit o the very right o't. It's all along o Zister. The Girl hath got a Hankering after this Son of a Whore of a Lord. I vound 'em together at my Cousin, my Lady *Bellaston*'s. He hath turned the Head o' her that's certain—but d—n me if he shall ha her—I'll ha no Lords nor Courtiers in my Vamily."

Western is equally passionate, within moments, in swearing that Sophia shall *not* have Jones, and that she *shall*. We are delighted by his stance, either way, and most delighted at his childish ease in moving from one position to the other without pause, embarrassment, or reflection. A passionate infant, Squire Western is sublime on the page, or on the screen, where as played by Hugh Griffith he ran off with the Osborne-Richardson *Tom Jones,* but in mere reality he would be a monster. As a representation he is triumphant because like the much greater Falstaff he is free of the superego. We rejoice in Western because he is freedom gone wild, including freedom from nasty plotting, yet his mindlessness almost frightens us.

Price is as accurate as ever when he observes that "Fielding controls his characters by limiting them," but Western is the grand exception, being out of control and extravagant, beyond all limits. No other eighteenth-century novel could accommodate Western, which is another indication of the power of *Tom Jones*. Something primeval in the mode of romance survives in Western the wild man, who hardly seems to belong to a post-Swiftian novel that still exalts the Augustan vision. Fielding, like Pope and Swift, joins the Enlightenment consciousness and ideas of order to an ongoing sense of the demands of energy. Johnson, who shared with Fielding the heritage of Pope and Swift, may have felt, obscurely but accurately, that Fielding, like Swift, gave too much away to the daemonic force of vitalism. "This kind of writing may be termed not improperly the Comedy of Romance," Johnson said of Fielding, thus relegating Fielding to the dark and enchanted ground not yet purified by reason. Johnson meant to condemn, perhaps, but guides us instead to Fielding's most surprising strength.

Fielding as Novelist: *Tom Jones*

Ian Watt

Literature yields few more interesting causes célèbres than the debate over the respective merits of the novels of Fielding and Richardson, a debate which continues today even though during the last century or so the supporters of Fielding have been in almost complete command of the field. The main reason for the vitality of the controversy is the exceptional range and variety of the issues—the opposition is not only between two kinds of novel, but between two kinds of physical and psychological constitution and between two social, moral and philosophical outlooks on life. Not only so: the dispute has the advantage of a spokesman whose strong and paradoxical support for Richardson acts as a perennial provocation to the supporters of Fielding, who are dismayed to find Dr. Johnson, the authoritative voice of neoclassicism, pronouncing anathema on the last full embodiment of the Augustan spirit in life and literature.

One way of resolving this last difficulty has been to suggest that Dr. Johnson's attitude should not be taken too seriously because it was dictated by friendship and personal obligation—Richardson had once saved him from being arrested for debt. Johnson's critical judgement, however, was not usually at the mercy of such considerations, and the supposition in any case runs counter to the fact that his enthusiastic endorsement of Richardson's novels was accompanied by a merciless awareness of the shortcomings of the man—witness his lethal jibe that Richardson "could not be content to sail quietly down the stream of

From *The Rise of the Novel*. © 1957 by Ian Watt. University of California Press, 1960.

reputation without longing to taste the froth from every stroke of the oar."

We should, then, consider Johnson's preference seriously, particularly in view of the consistency with which he recurred to his main charge. "All the difference between the characters of Fielding and those of Richardson," he maintained, according to Boswell, was that between "characters of manners," and "characters of nature." "Characters of manners," of course, Johnson ranked much lower on the grounds that although "very entertaining . . . they are to be understood by a more superficial observer than characters of nature, where a man must dive into the recesses of the human heart." This distinction between Richardson and Fielding was more memorably expressed when Johnson said that "there was as great a difference between them as between a man who knew how a watch was made, and a man who could tell the hour by looking on the dial plate"; and the same idea is present in the even more plainly invidious statement reported by Mrs. Thrale that "Richardson had picked the kernel of life . . . while Fielding was contented with the husk."

This basic distinction does not involve any direct divergence from critical orthodoxy, but it perhaps does so implicitly, since the basis of Richardson's "diving into the recesses of the human heart" was his detailed description of individual states of mind, a description which requires a minute particularity in the presentation of character, and which is therefore contrary to the usual neoclassical bias towards the general and the universal. There is no doubt that Johnson's theoretical presuppositions were strongly in this direction, as he often proclaimed the doctrine that the poet "must not dwell on the minuter distinctions by which one species differs from another." Yet his operative premises for fiction were apparently quite different, since he reproached Fielding for his reluctance to dwell on these very distinctions, telling Mrs. Thrale, for example, that "Fielding could describe a horse or an ass, but he never reached to a mule."

It would seem, then, that Johnson's vigorously independent literary sensibility tended to confirm at least one of the elements of the opposition described in the first chapter between neoclassical theory and the novel's formal realism. As for the discrepancy between Johnson's literary theory and his practical judgement, it need occasion little surprise: any body of doctrine is ambiguous in some of its applications, and especially when it is applied in areas for which it was not originally designed. In any case, Johnson's neoclassicism was not a simple thing (neither, for that matter, was neoclassicism); and his divergence from his usual principles in the present instance must surely be regarded as yet another example of how the radical honesty of his literary insight raised fundamental issues so forcibly that later criticism cannot but use his formulations as points of departure; any comparison between the two first masters of the novel form certainly must begin from the basis which he provided.

I

Tom Jones and *Clarissa* have sufficient similarity of theme to provide several closely parallel scenes which afford a concrete illustration of the differences between the methods of Fielding and Richardson as novelists. Both, for example, show us scenes where the heroine is forced to receive the addresses of the hated suitor their parents have chosen for them, and both also portray the later conflict between father and daughter which their refusal to marry this suitor provokes.

Here, first, is how Fielding describes the interview between Sophia Western and the odious Blifil:

> Mr. Blifil soon arrived; and Mr. Western soon after withdrawing, left the young couple together.
>
> Here a long silence of near a quarter of an hour ensued; for the gentleman, who was to begin the conversation, had all that unbecoming modesty which consists in bashfulness. He often attempted to speak, and as often suppressed his words just at the very point of utterance. At last, out they broke in a torrent of farfetched and high-strained compliments, which were answered on her side by downcast looks, half bows, and civil monosyllables.—Blifil, from his inexperience in the ways of women, and from his conceit of himself, took this behaviour for a modest assent to his courtship; and when, to shorten a scene which she could no longer support, Sophia rose up and left the room, he imputed that, too, merely to bashfulness, and comforted himself that he should soon have enough of her company.
>
> He was indeed perfectly well satisfied with his prospect of success; for as to that entire and absolute possession of the heart of his mistress, which romantic lovers require, the very idea of it never entered his head. Her fortune and her person were the sole objects of his wishes, of which he made no doubt

soon to obtain the absolute property; as Mr. Western's mind
was so earnestly bent on the match; and as he well knew the
strict obedience which Sophia was always ready to pay to her
father's will, and the greater still which her father would exact,
if there was occasion.

Structurally, the scene is based on that typical device of comedy, total
ignorance by one character of the intentions of the other as a result of a
misunderstanding between third parties—Squire Western has been mis-
led by the ineffable Mistress Western into thinking that Sophia loves
Blifil, not Tom Jones. It is perhaps because this misunderstanding must
be kept up that there is no actual conversation and little feeling of personal
contact between the characters concerned. Instead, Fielding, acting as
omniscient author, lets us into Blifil's mind, and the meanness of the
considerations by which it is governed: at the same time the consistent
irony of Fielding's tone suggests to us the probable limits of Blifil's role:
we need not fear that he will ever get possession of Sophia's fortune or
of her person, for, although he is cast as a villain, it is patently as the
villain in comedy.

Blifil's misunderstanding of Sophia's silence leads on to the next
comic complication, since it causes him to give Squire Western the
impression that his suit has prospered. Western at once goes to rejoice
with his daughter, who of course is unaware of how he has been deceived:

> Sophia, perceiving her father in this fit of affection, which she
> did not absolutely know the reason of (for fits of fondness were
> not unusual in him, though this was rather more violent than
> ordinary), thought she should never have a better second op-
> portunity of disclosing herself than at present, as far at least
> as regarded Mr. Blifil; and she too well foresaw the necessity
> which she should soon be under of coming to a full explana-
> tion. After having thanked the squire, therefore, for all his
> professions of kindness, she added with a look full of inex-
> pressible softness, "And is it possible that my papa can be so
> good as to place all his joy in his Sophy's happiness?" which
> Western having confirmed by a great oath and a kiss, she then
> laid hold of his hand, and falling on her knees, after many
> warm and passionate declarations of affection and duty, she
> begged him "not to make her the most miserable creature on
> earth, by forcing her to marry a man she detested. This I
> entreat of you, dear sir," said she, "for your sake, as well as

my own, since you are so very kind to tell me your happiness depends on mine."—"How! What!" says Western, staring wildly. "O, sir," continued she, "not only your poor Sophy's happiness, her very life, her being, depends upon your granting her request. I cannot live with Mr. Blifil. To force me into this marriage would be killing me."—"You can't live with Mr. Blifil!" says Mr. Western—"No, upon my soul, I can't," answered Sophia.—"Then die and be d—ned," cries he, spurning her from him . . . "I am resolved upon the match, and unless you consent to it, I will not give you a groat, not a single farthing; no, though I saw you expiring in the street, I would not relieve you with a morsel of bread. This is my fixed resolution, and so I leave you to consider on it." He then broke from her with such violence, that her face dashed against the floor; and he burst directly out of the room, leaving poor Sophia prostrate on the ground.

Fielding's primary aim is certainly not to reveal character through speech and action. We cannot be meant to deduce, for instance, that Sophia knows her father so poorly as to entertain any hopes of being able to hold him down to one position by force of logic; what Fielding tells us about Sophia's decision to break the matter to her father is obviously mainly aimed at heightening the comic reversal that is to follow. Similarly we cannot consider Western's threat—"No, though I saw you expiring in the street, I would not relieve you with a morsel of bread"—as characteristic of the man either in diction or sentiment—it is hackneyed trope that belongs to any such situation in melodrama, not to a particular Squire who habitually speaks the most uncouth Somersetshire jargon, and whose childish intemperateness is not elsewhere shown capable of such an imaginative flight. To say that Sophia's and Western's speeches are grossly out of character would be an exaggeration; but they are undoubtedly directed entirely towards exploiting the comic *volte-face* and not towards making us witnesses of an actual interview between a father and daughter in real life.

It is probably an essential condition for the realisation of Fielding's comic aim that the scene should not be rendered in all its physical and psychological detail; Fielding must temper our alarm for Sophia's fate by assuring us that we are witnessing, not real anguish, but that conventional kind of comic perplexity which serves to heighten our eventual pleasure at the happy ending, without in the meantime involving any unnecessary expenditure of tears on our part. Fielding's external and somewhat peremptory approach to his characters, in fact, would seem to be a necessary condition of the success of his main comic purpose: attention to the immediate counterpoint of misunderstanding and contradiction must not be dissipated by focussing interest on Sophia's feelings or on any other tangential issue.

A total contrast of purpose and method is offered by the way Richardson presents Clarissa's interview with Solmes, after her maid Hannah has warned her secretly that he is the husband that has been decided on for her. It is thus described in a letter to Anna Howe:

> I went down this morning when breakfast was ready with a very uneasy heart . . . wishing for an opportunity to appeal to my mother, in hopes to engage her interest in my behalf, and purposing to try to find one when she retired to her own apartment after breakfast; but, unluckily, there was the odious Solmes sitting asquat between my mother and sister, with *so much* assurance in his looks! But you know, my dear, that those we love not cannot do anything to please us.
>
> Had the wretch kept his seat, it might have been well enough: but the bent and broad-shouldered creature must needs rise and stalk towards a chair; which was just by that which was set for me.
>
> I removed it to a distance, as if to make way to my own: And down I sat, abruptly I believe; what I had heard all in my head.
>
> But this was not enough to daunt him. The man is a very confident, he is a very bold, staring man! Indeed, my dear, the man is very confident!
>
> He took the removed chair and drew it so near mine, squatting in it with his ugly weight, that he pressed upon my hoop. I was so offended (all I had heard, as I said, in my head) that I removed to another chair. I own I had too little command of myself. It gave my brother and sister too much advantage. I dare say they took it. But I did it involuntarily, I think. I could not help it. I knew not what I did.
>
> I saw that my father was excessively displeased. When angry, no man's countenance ever shows it so much as my father's. Clarissa Harlowe! said he with a big voice—and there he stopped. Sir! said I, trembling and curtsying (for I had not

then sat down again): and put my chair nearer the wretch, and sat down—my face, as I could feel, all in a glow.

Make tea, child, said my kind mamma: sit by me, love, and make tea.

I removed with pleasure to the seat the man had quitted; and being thus indulgently put into employment, soon recovered myself; and in the course of the breakfasting officiously asked two or three questions of Mr. Solmes, which I would not have done, but to make up with my father. *Proud spirits may be brought to!* whisperingly spoke my sister to me over her shoulder, with an air of triumph and scorn: but I did not mind her.

My mother was all kindness and condescension. I asked her once if she were pleased with the tea. . . .

Small incidents these, my dear, to trouble you with; only as they lead to greater, as you shall hear.

Before the usual breakfast-time was over my father withdrew with my mother, telling her he wanted to speak to her. Then my sister and next my aunt (who was with us) dropped away.

My brother gave himself some airs of insult, which I understood well enough; but which Mr. Solmes could make nothing of: and at last he arose from *his* seat. Sister, says he, I have a curiosity to show you. I will fetch it. And away he went; shutting the door close after him.

I saw what all this was for. I arose; the man hemming up for a speech, rising and beginning to set his splay feet (indeed, my dear, the man in all his ways is hateful to me!) in an approaching posture. I will save my brother the trouble of bringing to me his curiosity, said I. I curtsied—your servant, sir. The man cried, madam, madam, twice, and looked like a fool. But away I went—to find my brother to save my word. But my brother, indifferent as the weather was, was gone to walk in the garden with my sister. A plain case that he had left his *curiosity* with me, and designed to show me no other.

This passage is characteristic of Richardson's very different kind of realism. Clarissa is describing what happened "this morning," and is "as minute as" she knows Anna wishes her to be; only so can Richardson convey the physical reality of the scene—the party at breakfast, the jockeying for position over trifles, and all the ordinarily trivial domestic details which bear the main burden of the drama. The letter form gives Richardson access to thoughts and emotions of a kind that cannot issue in speech, and are hardly capable of rational analysis—the flux and reflux of Clarissa's lacerated sensibility as she struggles against parental tyranny on the battlefield of petty circumstance: as a result we have quite a different kind of participation from that which Fielding produces: not a lively but objective sense of the total comic pattern, but a complete identification with the consciousness of Clarissa while her nerves still quiver from the recollection of the scene, and her imagination recoils from the thought of her own strained alternation between involuntary revolt and paralysed compliance.

Because Richardson's narrative sequence is based on an exploration in depth of the protagonist's reaction to experience, it encompasses many minor shades of emotion and character that are not found in the passages from *Tom Jones*. Fielding does not attempt to do more than to make us understand the rational grounds on which Sophia acts as she does—there is nothing which would not fit almost any sensible young girl's behaviour in the circumstances: whereas Richardson's epistolary technique, and the intimacy of Clarissa with Anna, encourages him to go far beyond this, and communicate a host of things which deepen and particularise our picture of Clarissa's total moral being. Her shuddering ejaculation—"Indeed, my dear, the man is very confident," her scornful comment on her sister's intervention—"I did not mind her," and her admission of involvement in petty family rivalries—she regrets moving away from Solmes because "It gave my brother and sister too much advantage"—all these details of characterisation must surely be overlooked by those who describe Richardson as a creator of "ideal" characters: there is, of course, great will and tenacity in Clarissa, but it is very definitely that of an inexperienced young woman, who has her fair share of sisterly vindictiveness and pert self-assertion, and who, far from being an idealised figure of virgin sainthood, is capable of the catty and sardonic emphasis on Mr. Solmes as a "curiosity." Nor is she by any means a disembodied being; we have no indications of any physical reaction on Sophia's part towards Blifil, but we are given Clarissa's very intense one to Solmes— an instinctive sexual revulsion from "his ugly weight."

The same setting of personal relationships in a minutely described physical, psychological and even physiological continuum is shown in the brief scene which is the counterpart of the second passage quoted from *Tom Jones*. After two private interviews with her mother, Clarissa has been faced with a family ultimatum, and her mother is with her to receive an answer:

> Just then, up came my father, with a sternness in his looks that made me tremble. He took two or three turns about my chamber, though pained by his gout. And then said to my mother, who was silent, as soon as she saw him:
>
> My dear, you are long absent. Dinner is near ready. What you had to say lay in a very little compass. Surely, you have nothing to do but to declare *your* will, and *my* will—but perhaps you may be talking of the preparations. Let us soon have you down—your daughter in your hand, if worthy of the name.
>
> And down he went, casting his eye upon me with a look so stern that I was unable to say one word to him, or even for a few minutes to my mother.

Richardson and Fielding portray the cruelty of the two fathers very differently; that of Squire Western has an involuntary and exaggerated quality, whereas Mr. Harlowe's is that of ordinary life; the latter's callous resolve seems all the more convincing because it is only manifested in his refusal to speak to Clarissa—our own emotional involvement in the inner world of Clarissa makes it possible for a father's silent look to have a resonance that is quite lacking in the physical and rhetorical hyperbole by which Fielding demonstrates the fury of Squire Western.

II

On further analysis, then, it appears that Johnson's comparison between Richardson and Fielding does not directly raise the question of which was the better psychologist, but depends rather on their quite opposite literary intentions: those of Fielding allotted characterisation a much less important place in his total literary structure, and precluded him even from attempting the effects which were suited to Richardson's very different aim. The full implications of the divergence can perhaps be most clearly and inclusively demonstrated in Fielding's handling of the plot in *Tom Jones,* for it reflects the whole of his social, moral and literary outlook.

Fielding's conduct of the action, despite a few excrescences such as the interpolated story of the Man of the Hill, and some signs of haste and confusion in the concluding books, exhibits a remarkably fine control over a very complicated structure, and abundantly justifies Coleridge's famous eulogy: "What a master of composition Fielding was! Upon my word, I think the *Oedipus Tyrannus, The Alchemist,* and *Tom Jones,* the three most perfect plots ever planned."

Perfect for what? we must ask. Not, certainly, for the exploration of character and of personal relations, since in all three plots the emphasis falls on the author's skillfully contrived revelation of an external and deterministic scheme: in *Oedipus* the hero's character is of minor importance compared with the consequences of his past actions, which were themselves the result of a prophecy made long before his birth; in *The Alchemist* the portrayal of Face and Subtle does not go far beyond the need for suitable instruments to carry out Jonson's complex series of chicaneries; while the plot of *Tom Jones* offers a combination of these features. As in Sophocles, the crucial secret, that of the hero's actual birth, is very elaborately prepared for and hinted at throughout the action, and its eventual disclosure brings about the final reordering of all the main issues of the story: while, as in Jonson, this final reordering is achieved through the unmasking of a complicated pattern of villainy and deception.

The three plots are alike in another respect: their basic direction is towards a return to the norm, and they therefore have a fundamentally static quality. In this they no doubt reflect the conservatism of their authors, a conservatism which in Fielding's case is probably connected with the fact that he belonged, not to the trading class like Defoe and Richardson, but to the gentry. The plots of the novels of Defoe and Richardson, as we have seen, mirrored certain dynamic tendencies in the outlook of their class: in *Moll Flanders,* for example, money has a certain autonomous force which determines the action at every turn. In *Tom Jones,* on the other hand, as in *The Alchemist,* money is something that the good characters either have or are given or momentarily lose: only bad characters devote any effort either to getting it or keeping it. Money, in fact, is a useful plot device but it has no controlling significance.

Birth, on the other hand, has a very different status in *Tom Jones*: as a determining factor in the plot it is almost the equivalent of money in Defoe or virtue in Richardson. In this emphasis, of course, Fielding reflects the general tenor of the social thought of his day: the basis of society is and should be a system of classes each with their own capacities and responsibilities. The vigour of Fielding's satire on the upper classes, for example, should not be interpreted as the expression of any egalitarian tendency: it is really a tribute to the firmness of his belief in the class premise. It is true that in *Amelia* he goes so far as to say that "of all kinds of pride, there is none so unChristian as that of station." But that, of course, is only a matter of noblesse oblige; and in *Tom Jones* Fielding also wrote that "liberality of spirits" was a quality which he had "scarce ever seen in men of low birth and education."

This class fixity is an essential part of *Tom Jones*. Tom may think it unfortunate that, as a foundling of presumed low ancestry, he cannot marry Sophia; but he does not question the propriety of the assumption on which their separation is decreed. The ultimate task of Fielding's plot therefore is to unite the lovers without subverting the basis of the social order; and this can only be done by revealing that Mr. Jones, though illegitimate, is genteel. This, however, is not wholly a surprise to the perceptive reader, for whom Tom's eminent "liberality of spirit" has already suggested his superior pedigree; the recent Soviet critic, therefore, who sees the story as the triumph of a proletarian hero is neglecting, not only the facts of his birth, but its continuing implications for his character.

Fielding's conservatism accounts for another and much more general difference between the plots of *Tom Jones* and *Clarissa*: for whereas Richardson depicts the crucifixion of the individual by society, Fielding portrays the successful adaptation of the individual to society, and this entails a very different relation between plot and character.

In *Clarissa* the individual must be given priority in the total structure: Richardson merely brings together certain individuals, and their proximity is all that is necessary to set off an extended chain reaction which then proceeds under its own impetus and modifies all the characters and their mutual relationships. In *Tom Jones,* on the other hand, society and the larger order which it represents must have priority, and the plot's function, therefore, is to perform a physical rather than a chemical change: it acts as a kind of magnet that pulls every individual particle out of the random order brought about by temporal accident and human imperfection and puts them all back into their proper position. The constitution of the particles themselves—the characters—is not modified in the process, but the plot serves to reveal something much more important—the fact that all human particles are subject to an ultimate invisible force which exists in the universe whether they are there to show it or not.

Such a plot reflects the general literary strategy of neoclassicism; just as the creation of a field of force makes visible the universal laws of magnetism, so the supreme task of the writer was to make visible in the human scene the operations of universal order—to unveil the handiwork of Pope's "Unerring Nature, still divinely bright, / One clear, unchanged and universal light."

This much wider perspective on character obviously reduces the importance which will be attached to the nature and actions of any particular individual entity—they are mainly interesting as manifestations of the great pattern of Nature. This informs Fielding's treatment of every aspect of characterisation—not only the extent to which his dramatis personae are individualised, but the degree of attention paid to their subjective lives, to their moral development, and to their personal relationships.

Fielding's primary objectives in the portrayal of character are clear but limited: to assign them to their proper category by giving as few diagnostic features as are necessary for the task. Such was his conception of "invention" or "creation": "a quick and sagacious penetration into the true essence of all the objects of our contemplation." This meant in practice that once the individual had been appropriately labelled the author's only remaining duty was to see that he continued to speak and act consistently. As Aristotle put it in the *Poetics,* "character" is "that which reveals the moral purpose," and consequently "speeches . . . which do not make this manifest . . . are not expressive of character." Parson Supple must never cease to be supple.

So it is that Fielding does not make any attempt to individualise his characters. Allworthy is sufficiently categorised by his name, while that of Tom Jones, compounded as it is out of two of the commonest names in the language, tells us that we must regard him as the representative of manhood in general, in accordance with his creator's purpose to show "not men, but manners; not an individual, but a species."

The scope of the word "manners" has dwindled so drastically in the last few centuries—no doubt as a result of the way individualism has reduced the areas in which identity of thought and action is generally expected—that the phrase "characters of manners" no longer means very much. It can perhaps be best explained in terms of the contrast with Richardson's "characters of nature." Richardson's literary objective, as B. W. Downs has pointed out, is not so much character—the stable elements in the individual's mental and moral constitution—as personality: he does not analyse Clarissa, but presents a complete and detailed behavioural report on her whole being: she is defined by the fullness of our participation in her life. Fielding's purpose, on the other hand, is analytic: he is not interested in the exact configuration of motives in any particular person's mind at any particular time but only in those features of the individual which are necessary to assign him to his moral and social species. He therefore studies each character in the light of his general knowledge of human behaviour, of "manners," and anything purely individual is of no taxonomic value. Nor is there any need to look inside: if, as Johnson said, Fielding gives us the husk, it is because the surface alone is usually quite sufficient to identify the specimen—the expert does not need to assay the kernel.

There are many other reasons for Fielding's predominantly external approach to character, reasons of a social and philosophical as well as of a literary order. To begin with, the opposite approach involved a breach of decorum: as Fielding's cousin Lady Mary Wortley Montagu pointed out, it was very bad manners for Richardson's heroines to "declare all they think," since "fig leaves are as necessary for our minds as our bodies." It was also consistent with the classical tradition as a whole, as we have seen, to avoid the intimate and confessional approach to personality; and in any case the philosophical problems of self-consciousness had only begun to receive attention some six centuries after Aristotle in the works of Plotinus. Lastly, as was evident in the treatment of Blifil and Sophia, Fielding's comic purpose itself required an external approach, and for a compelling reason. If we identify ourselves with the characters we shall not be in any mood to appreciate the humour of the larger comedy in which they are risible participants: life, we have been told, is a comedy only to the man who thinks, and the comic author must not make us feel every stroke of the lash as his characters squirm under his corrective rod.

At all events, Fielding avowedly and even ostentatiously refused to go too deep into the minds of his characters, on the general grounds that "it is our province to relate facts, and we shall leave causes to persons of much higher genius." We have noted how little was said about the feelings, as opposed to the rational determinations, of Blifil and Sophia. This was quite conscious on Fielding's part: he had already remarked ironically of Blifil that "it would be an ill office in us to pay a visit to the inmost recesses of his mind, as some scandalous people search into the most secret affairs of their friends, and often pry into their closets and cupboards, only to discover their poverty and meanness to the world"; similarly when Fielding came to present Sophia's feelings when she first learned of Tom's love, he excused himself in the words: "as to the present situation of her mind I shall adhere to the rule of Horace, by not attempting to describe it, from despair of success."

Fielding's avoidance of the subjective dimension, then, is quite intentional: but that does not, of course, mean that it has no drawbacks, for it undoubtedly has, and they become very apparent whenever important emotional climaxes are reached. Coleridge, for all his love of Fielding, pointed out that in the soliloquies between Sophia and Tom Jones before their final reconciliation, nothing could be "more forced and unnatural: the language is without vivacity or spirit, the whole matter is incongruous, and totally devoid of psychological truth." In fact, Fielding merely gave us a stock comic scene: elevated sentiments of penitent ardour on the hero's part were countered by wronged womanhood's equally elevated scorn of her faithless suitor. Soon after, of course, Sophia accepts Tom, and we are surprised by her very sudden and unexplained reversal: the dénouement has been given a certain comic life, but at the expense of the reality of emotions involved.

This emotional artificiality is very general in *Tom Jones*. When the hero, for instance, is expelled from Allworthy's house we are told that "he presently fell into the most violent agonies, tearing his hair from his head, and using most other actions which generally accompany fits of madness, rage and despair"; and later that he read Sophia's parting letter "a hundred times over, and kissed it a hundred times as often." Fielding's use of these hackneyed hyperboles to vouch for the intensity of the emotions of his characters underlines the price that he pays for his comic approach: it denies him a convincing and continuous access to the inner life of his characters, so that whenever he has to exhibit their emotional life, he can only do it externally by making them have exaggerated physical reactions.

The fact that Fielding's characters do not have a convincing inner life means that their possibilities of psychological development are very limited. Tom Jones's character, for example, exhibits some development, but it is of a very general kind. Tom's early imprudences, his youthful lack of worldly wisdom, and his healthy animality, for example, lead to his disgrace, his expulsion from the Allworthy household, his subsequent difficulties on the road and in London, and his apparently irrecoverable loss of Sophia's love. At the same time his good qualities, his courage, honour and benevolence, all of which have been glimpsed at the beginning, eventually combine to extricate him from the nadir of his misfortunes, and restore him to the love and respect of those who surround him. But although different qualities come to the fore at different times they have all been present from the beginning, and we have not been taken close enough to Tom's mind to be able to do anything but take on trust Fielding's implication, which is that his hero will be able to control his weaknesses by the wisdom he has learned of experience.

In taking this essentially static view of human nature Fielding was following the time-hallowed Aristotelian view, which was actually held with much greater rigidity by most of the philosophers and literary critics of his time. It is, of course, an ahistorical view of character, as Fielding showed in *Joseph Andrews,* when he asserted that his characters were "taken from the life," but added that the particular lawyer in question was "not only alive, but hath been so this four thousand years." It follows logically that if human nature is essentially stable, there is no need to detail the processes whereby any one example of it has reached its full development; such processes are but temporary and superficial modifications of a moral constitution which is unalterably fixed from birth. Such, for example, is the premise of the way that although Tom and Blifil share the same mother and are brought up in the same household by the same tutors, their respective courses are unalterably set in different directions from the very beginning.

Once again the contrast with Richardson is complete. Much of our sense of Clarissa's psychological development arises from the way that her experience brings a continual deepening of her understanding of her own past: as a result character and plot are indivisible. Tom Jones, on the other hand, is not in touch with his own past at all: we feel a certain unreality in his actions because they always seem to be spontaneous reactions to stimuli that the plot has been manipulated to provide; we have no sense that they are manifestations of a developing moral life. We cannot but feel surprise, for instance, when, immediately after accepting fifty pounds from Lady Bellaston, Tom gives his famous lecture to Nightingale on sexual ethics. It is not that the two actions are inherently contradictory—Tom's ethics have throughout been based on the much greater heinousness of harming others than of failing to live up to one's moral code oneself; but if we had been given some indication that Tom was aware of the apparent contradictions between his speech and his own past practice he might have sounded less priggish and more convincing. Actually, of course, separate parts of Tom's nature can hold very little converse with each other, because there is only one agency for such converse—the individual consciousness through which the whole repertoire of past actions operates—and Fielding does not take us into this consciousness because he believes that individual character is a specific combination of stable and separate predispositions to action, rather than the product of its own past.

For the same reasons personal relationships are also relatively unimportant in *Tom Jones.* If there is a controlling force independent of the individual actors and their positions with respect to each other, and if their own characters are innate and unchanging, there is no reason why Fielding should give close attention to their mutual feelings, since they cannot play a decisive role. Here, again, the scene between Sophia and Blifil was typical in that it reflected the extent to which the structure of *Tom Jones* as a whole depends on the lack of any effective communication between the characters: just as Blifil must misunderstand Sophia, so Allworthy must fail to see Blifil in his true light, and Tom must be unable either to understand Blifil's true nature or to explain himself properly either to Allworthy or Sophia until the closing scenes. For, since Fielding's view of human life and his general literary purpose did not permit him to subordinate his plot to the deepening exploration of personal relationships, he needed a structure based on an elaborate counterpoint of deception and surprise, and this would be impossible if the characters could share each other's minds and take their fates into their own hands.

There is, then, an absolute connection in *Tom Jones* between the treatment of plot and of character. Plot has priority, and it is therefore plot which must contain the elements of complication and development. Fielding achieves this by superimposing on a central action that is, in essentials as simple as that in *Clarissa,* a very complex series of relatively autonomous subplots and episodes which are in the nature of dramatic variations on the main theme. These relatively independent narrative units are combined in a concatenation whose elaboration and symmetry is suggested in the most obvious outward aspect of the book's formal order: unlike the novels of Defoe and Richardson, *Tom Jones* is carefully divided into compositional units of different sizes—some two hundred chapters which are themselves grouped into eighteen books disposed into three groups of six, dealing respectively with the early lives, the journeys to London, and the activities on arrival, of the main characters.

This extreme diversification of the narrative texture reinforces, of course, Fielding's tendency not to dwell for long on any one scene or character. In the passages quoted, for example, there was none of the intensive treatment which Richardson gave to Clarissa's interview with Solmes; most of Fielding's time was spent on making clear the initial misunderstanding, and the scale of the scene allowed no more in the way of characterisation than a designing hypocrite, a trapped maiden and a heavy father. But even if there had been any full absorption in the feelings of Sophia, for example, it would soon have been terminated by the management of the ensuing scenes: for, just as we left Sophia immediately after Squire Western had stormed out of the room, and were thus spared any prolonged awareness of her sufferings, so in the next chapter our attention was soon switched away from her parting interview with Tom Jones by Fielding's announcement that "the scene, which I believe some of my readers will think had lasted long enough, was interrupted by one of so different a nature, that we shall reserve the relation of it for a different chapter."

This is typical of the narrative mode of *Tom Jones*: the author's commentary makes no secret of the fact that his aim is not to immerse us wholly in his fictional world, but rather to show the ingenuity of his own inventive resources by contriving an amusing counterpoint of scenes and characters; quick changes are the essence of Fielding's comic manner, and a new chapter will always bring a new situation for the characters, or present different characters in a similar scene for ironical contrast. In addition, by a great variety of devices, of which the chapter headings are usually significant pointers, our attention is continually drawn to the fact that the ultimate cohesive force of the book resides not in the characters and their relationships, but in an intellectual and literary structure which has a considerable degree of autonomy.

The effects of this procedure and its relationship to Fielding's treatment of character can be summarised in relation to a brief scene which occurs after Tom has heard that Allworthy is to recover from his illness. He takes a walk "in a most delicious grove," and contemplates the cruelty of fortune which separates him from his beloved Sophia:

> Was I but possessed of thee, one only suit of rags thy whole estate, is there a man on earth whom I would envy! How contemptible would the brightest Circassian beauty, dressed in all the jewels of the Indies, appear to my eyes! But why do I mention another woman? Could I think my eyes capable of looking at any other with tenderness, these hands should tear them from my head. No, my Sophia, if cruel fortune separates us for ever, my soul shall dote on thee alone. The chastest constancy will I ever preserve to thy image. . . .
>
> At these words he started up and beheld—not his Sophia— no, nor a Circassian maid richly and elegantly attired for the grand Signior's seraglio

but Molly Seagrim, with whom, "after a parley" which Fielding omits, Tom retires to "the thickest part of the grove."

The least convincing aspect of the episode is the diction: the speech habits manifested here obviously bear little relation to those we expect of Tom Jones. But, of course, they are a stylistic necessity for Fielding's immediate purpose—the comic deflation of the heroic and romantic pretences of the human word by the unheroic and unromantic eloquence of the human deed. Tom Jones is no more than a vehicle for the expression of Fielding's skepticism about lovers' vows; and he must be made to speak in terms that parody the high-flown rhetoric of the pastoral romance to give point to the succeeding wayside encounter which belongs to the very different world of the *pastourelle*. Nor can Fielding pause to detail the psychological processes whereby Tom is metamorphosed from Sophia's romantic lover to Moll's prompt gallant: to illustrate the commonplace that "actions speak louder than words," the actions must be very silent and they must follow very hard upon very loud words.

The relation of this episode to the larger structure of the novel is typical. One of Fielding's general organising themes is the proper place of sex in human life; this encounter neatly illustrates the conflicting tendencies of headstrong youth, and shows that Tom has not yet reached the continence of moral adulthood. The scene, therefore, plays its part in the general moral and intellectual scheme; and it is also significantly connected with the workings of the plot, since Tom's lapse eventually becomes a factor in his dismissal by Allworthy, and therefore leads to the ordeals which eventually make him a worthier mate for Sophia.

At the same time Fielding's treatment of the scene is also typical in avoiding any detailed presentation of Tom's feelings either at the time or later—to take his hero's faithlessness too seriously would jeopardise Fielding's primarily comic intention in the episode, and he therefore manipulates it in such a way as to discourage us from giving it a significance which it might have in ordinary life. Comedy, and especially comedy on an elaborate scale, often involves this kind of limited liability to psychological interpretation: it applies to Blifil's malice and to Sophia's sufferings in the scenes quoted earlier, and Allworthy's sudden illness and recovery, which have led to Tom's lapse, must be placed in the same perspective. We must not dwell on the apparent fact that Allworthy is incapable of distinguishing between a cold and a mortal illness, since we are not intended to draw the implications for his character that he is either an outrageous hypochondriac or lamentably unskilled in choosing physicians: Allworthy's illness is only a diplomatic chill, and we must not infer anything from it except a shift in Fielding's narrative policy.

Tom Jones, then, would seem to exemplify a principle of considerable significance for the novel form in general: namely, that the importance of the plot is in inverse proportion to that of character. This principle has an interesting corollary: the organisation of the narrative into an extended and complex formal structure will tend to turn the protagonists into its passive agents, but it will offer compensatingly greater opportunities for the introduction of a variety of minor characters, whose treatment will not be hampered in the same way by the roles which they are allotted by the complications of the narrative design.

The principle and its corollary would seem to lie behind Coleridge's contrast of the "forced and unnatural quality" of the scenes between the protagonists in *Tom Jones* and Fielding's treatment of the "characters of postilions, landlords, landladies, waiters" where "nothing can be more true, more happy or more humorous." These minor characters figure only in scenes which require exactly the amount of psychological individuality which they are possessed of; relieved of any responsibility for carrying out the major narrative design Mrs. Honour can get herself dismissed from the Western household by methods which are at once triumphantly comic, sociologically perceptive and eminently characteristic, nor is there any question of the violence to character and probability which colours the ways whereby Tom Jones, for example, or Sophia leave home.

Such is the pattern of most comic novels with elaborate plots, from Fielding and Smollett to Dickens: the creative emphasis is on characters who are minor at least in the sense that they are not deeply involved in the working out of the plot; whereas the Tom Jones's, the Roderick Randoms and the David Copperfields are less convincing as characters because their personalities bear little direct relation to the part they must play, and some of the actions in which the plot involves them suggests a weakness or folly which is probably at variance with the actual intentions of their author towards them.

On the other hand, the type of novel which is perhaps most typical of the genre, and which achieves effects which have not been duplicated in any other literary form, has used a very different kind of plot. From Sterne and Jane Austen to Proust and Joyce the Aristotelian priority of plot over character has been wholly reversed, and a new type of formal structure has been evolved in which the plot attempts only to embody the ordinary processes of life and in so doing becomes wholly dependent on the characters and the development of their relationships. It is Defoe and above all Richardson who provide this tradition with its archetypes, just as it is Fielding who provides that for the opposite tradition.

III

Johnson's most famous criticism of Fielding's novels is concerned with their basic technique, but from his own point of view it was probably their moral shortcomings which were the decisive factor. It is certainly this with which he was concerned in his only published reference to Fielding, although even here it is only by implication. In the *Rambler* (1750) Johnson attacked the effects of "familiar histories" whose wicked heroes were made so attractive that "we lose abhorrence of their faults," apparently with *Roderick Random* (1748) and *Tom Jones* (1749) chiefly in mind. He certainly later told Hannah More that he "scarcely knew a more corrupt work" than *Tom Jones,* and, on the other hand, praised *Clarissa* on the significant grounds that "It was in the power of Richardson alone to teach us at once esteem and detestation; to make virtuous resentment overpower all the benevolence which wit, elegance, and courage naturally excite, and to lose at last the hero in the villain."

We find it difficult today to share much of Johnson's abhorrence of the morality of *Tom Jones* and are, indeed, more likely to be unjust to Richardson, and to assume without question that his concern, and that of his heroines, for feminine chastity, can only be explained by prurience on his part or hypocrisy on theirs. But this may not be so, and, conversely, we must in fairness recognise that there are many moral offences in *Tom Jones* which receive a much more tolerant treatment than any Puritan moralist would have accorded them. Defoe and Richardson, for example, are unsparing in their denunciation of drunkenness; but when Tom Jones gets drunk in his joy at Allworthy's recovery, Fielding shows no reprobation: it is admittedly an imprudence which later contributes to the hero's expulsion, but Fielding's only direct comment is a humorous editorial development of the *in vino veritas* commonplace.

It is the sexual issue, however, which is crucial, both in the moral scheme of *Tom Jones,* and in the objections of its critics. Fielding certainly does not endorse his hero's incontinence, and Tom himself admits that he has been "faulty" in this respect; but the general tendency throughout the novel is surely to qualify the condemnation and make unchastity appear a venial sin—even the good Mrs. Miller, for example, seems to think she has put a fairly good face on matters by pleading to Sophia that Tom has "never been guilty of a single instance of infidelity to her since . . . seeing her in town."

Fielding's plot obviously does not punish the sexual transgressions either of Tom Jones or of the many other characters who are guilty in this respect so severely as Richardson, for example, would have wished. Even in *Amelia,* where Booth's adultery is both more serious in itself than anything that can be charged against Tom Jones, and is treated much more severely by Fielding, the plot eventually rescues Booth from the consequences of his acts. There is therefore considerable justification for Ford Madox Ford's denunciation of "fellows like Fielding, and to some extent Thackeray, who pretend that if you are a gay drunkard, lecher, squanderer of your goods and fumbler in placket holes you will eventually find a benevolent uncle, concealed father or benefactor who will shower on you bags of ten thousands of guineas, estates, and the hands of adorable mistresses—these fellows are dangers to the body politic and horribly bad constructors of plots."

Ford, of course, chooses to disregard both Fielding's positive moral intentions and the tendency of comic plots in general to achieve a happy ending at the cost of certain lenity in the administration of justice. For—although Fielding was long regarded as something of a debauchee himself and did not indeed have full justice done to his literary greatness until scholarship had cleared him of the charges made by contemporary gossip and repeated by his first biographer, Murphy—Fielding was in fact as much of a moralist as Richardson, although of a different kind. He believed that virtue, far from being the result of the suppression of instinct at the behest of public opinion, was itself a natural tendency to goodness or benevolence. In Tom Jones he tried to show a hero possessed of a virtuous heart, but also of the lustiness and lack of deliberation to which natural goodness was particularly prone, and which easily led to error and even to vice. To realise his moral aim, therefore, Fielding had to show how the good heart was threatened by many dangers in its hazardous course to maturity and knowledge of the world; yet, at the same time and without exculpating his hero, he had also to show that although Tom's moral transgressions were a likely and perhaps even a necessary stage in the process of moral growth, they did not betoken a vicious disposition; even Tom Jones's carefree animality has a generous quality that is lacking in Clarissa's self-centred and frigid virtue. The happy conclusion of the story, therefore, is very far from representing the kind of moral and literary confusion which Ford alleges, and is actually the culmination of Fielding's moral and literary logic.

The contrast between Fielding and Richardson as moralists is heightened by the effects of their very different narrative points of view. Richardson focusses attention on the individual, and whatever virtue or vice he is dealing with will loom very large, and have all its implications reflected in the action: Fielding, on the other hand, deals with too many characters and too complicated a plot to give the single individual virtue or vice quite this importance.

Besides this tendency of the plot, it is also part of Fielding's intention as a moralist to put every phenomenon into its larger perspective. Sexual virtue and sexual vice, for example, are placed in a broad moral perspective, and the results do not always produce the kind of emphasis that the sexual reformer would wish. Fielding knows, for example, and wishes to show, that some marriage designs may be more vicious than the most abandoned profligacy: witness Blifil whose "designs were strictly honourable as the phrase is, that is to rob a lady of her fortune by marriage." He knows, too, that moral indignation against promiscuity is not necessarily the result of a real love of virtue: witness the passage in which we are told that "to exclude all vulgar concubinage, and to drive all whores in rags from within the walls is within the power of everyone. This my landlady very strictly adhered to, and this her virtuous guests, who did not travel in rags, would very reasonably have expected from her." Here Fielding's Swiftian suavity reminds us of the cruelty and injustice with which complacent virtue is too often associated; but a narrow-minded moralist might see behind the irony a shocking failure to condemn "whores in rags," and even, perhaps, an implicit sympathy for them.

Fielding, then, attempts to broaden our moral sense rather than to intensify its punitive operations against licentiousness. But, at the same time, his function as the voice of traditional social morality means that his attitude to sexual ethics is inevitably normative; it certainly does not, as Boswell said, "encourage a strained and rarely possible virtue," but rather reflects, as Leslie Stephen put it, "the code by which men of sense generally govern their conduct, as distinguished from that by which they affect to be governed in language." Aristotle's Golden Mean is often, perhaps, capable of a certain subversion of rigid ethical principles: and it is perhaps as a good Aristotelian that Fielding comes very close to suggesting that too much chastity in Blifil is as bad as Tom's too little.

There is a further reason why Johnson, who was, after all, an ethical rigorist in his own way, should have found *Tom Jones* a corrupt work. Comedy—if only to maintain an atmosphere of good-humour between audience and participants—often involves a certain complicity in acts and sentiments which we might not treat so tolerantly in ordinary life. Perhaps the most insistent note in *Tom Jones* is Fielding's worldly-wise good-humour, and it often persuades us to regard sexual irregularities as ludicrous rather than wicked.

Mrs. Fitzpatrick, for instance, is dismissed with the words: "she lives in reputation at the polite end of town, and is so good an economist that she spends three times the income of her fortune without running into debt." Mrs. Fitzpatrick must remain true to character, and yet be included in the happy ending; nor can Fielding upset the conviviality of his final meeting with his readers to express his abhorrence at the lamentable source of income which we must surmise for his character.

On other occasions, of course, Fielding's humour on that perennial comic resource, sex, is much more overt: in *Jonathan Wilde*, for example, when the captain of the ship asks the hero "if he had no more Christianity in him than to ravish a woman in a storm?" or in *Tom Jones* when Mrs. Honour gives her celebrated retort to Sophia's "Would you not, Honour, fire a pistol at any one who should attack your virtue?"—"To be sure, ma'am, . . . one's virtue is a dear thing, especially to us poor servants; for it is our livelihood, as a body may say: yet I mortally hate firearms." There is, of course, the same broadening tendency in Fielding's humour here as in his treatment of moral issues in general: we must not forget that even the most virtuous indignation is capable of elementary logical fallacies, or that humankind's allegiance to virtue is capable of cautious afterthoughts. But the tacit assumption of much of Fielding's humour is surely one which suggests that "broad-mindedness" in its modern sense, which typically tends to have a sexual reference, is part of the expansion of sympathy to which his novels as a whole invite us: a relish for wholesome bawdy, in fact, is a necessary part of the moral education of a sex-bedevilled humanity: such, at least, was the classical role of comedy, and Fielding was perhaps the last great writer who continued that tradition.

IV

As far as most modern readers are concerned it is not Fielding's moral but his literary point of view which is open to objection. For his conception of his role is that of a guide who, not content with taking us "behind the scenes of this great theatre of nature," feels that he must explain everything which is to be found there; and such authorial intrusion, of course, tends to diminish the authenticity of his narrative.

Fielding's personal intrusion into *Tom Jones* begins with his dedication to the Honourable George Lyttleton, a dedication, it must be admitted, which goes far to justify Johnson's definition of this form of writing—"a servile address to a patron." There are numerous further references in the body of his work to others among Fielding's patrons, notably Ralph Allen and Lord Chancellor Hardwicke, not to mention other acquaintances whom Fielding wished to compliment, including one of his surgeons, Mr. John Ranby, and various innkeepers.

The effect of these references is certainly to break the spell of the imaginary world represented in the novel: but the main interference with the autonomy of this world comes from Fielding's introductory chapters, containing literary and moral essays, and even more from his frequent discussions and asides to the reader within the narrative itself. There is no doubt that Fielding's practice here leads him in completely the opposite direction from Richardson, and converts the novel into a social and indeed into a sociable literary form. Fielding brings us into a charmed circle composed, not only of the fictional characters, but also of Fielding's friends and of his favourites among the poets and moralists of the past. He is, indeed, almost as attentive to his audience as to his characters, and his narrative, far from being an intimate drama which we peep at through a keyhole, is a series of reminiscences told by a genial raconteur in some wayside inn—the favoured and public locus of his tale.

This approach to the novel is quite consistent with Fielding's major intention—it promotes a distancing effect which prevents us from being so fully immersed in the lives of the characters that we lose our alertness to the larger implications of their actions—implications which Fielding brings out in his capacity of omniscient chorus. On the other hand, Fielding's interventions obviously interfere with any sense of narrative illusion, and break with almost every narrative precedent, beginning with that set by Homer, whom Aristotle praised for saying "very little *in propria persona,*" and for maintaining elsewhere the attitude either of a dispassionate narrator, or of an impersonator of one of the characters.

Few readers would like to be without the prefatory chapters, or Fielding's diverting asides, but they undoubtedly derogate from the reality of the narrative: as Richardson's friend, Thomas Edwards, wrote, "we see every moment" that it is Fielding who "does *personam gerere,*" whereas Richardson is "the thing itself." So, although Fielding's garrulity about his characters and his conduct of the action initiated a popular practice in the English novel, it is not surprising that it has been condemned by most modern critics, and on these grounds. Ford Madox Ford, for instance, complained that the "trouble with the English nuvvelist from Fielding to Meredith, is that not one of them cares whether you believe in their characters or not," and Henry James was shocked by the way Trollope, and other "accomplished novelists," concede "in a digression, a parenthesis or an aside" that their fiction is "only make-believe." James went on to lay down the central principle of the novelist's attitude to his creation, which is very similar to that described above as inherent in formal realism: Trollope, and any novelist who shares his attitude, James says,

> admits that the events he narrates have not really happened, and that he can give the narrative any turn the reader may like best. Such a betrayal of a sacred office seems to me, I confess, a terrible crime; it is what I mean by the attitude of apology, and it shocks me every whit as much in Trollope as it would have shocked me in Gibbon or Macaulay. It implies that the novelist is less occupied in looking for the truth (the truth of course I mean, that he assumes, the premises that we must grant him, whatever they may be) than the historian, and in so doing it deprives him at a stroke of all his standing room.

There is not, of course, any doubt as to Fielding's intention of "looking for the truth"—he tells us indeed in *Tom Jones* that "we determined to guide our pen throughout by the directions of truth." But he perhaps underestimated the connection between truth and the maintenance of the reader's "historical faith." This, at least, is the suggestion of a passage towards the end of *Tom Jones* when he proclaims that he will let his hero be hanged rather than extricate him from his troubles by unnatural means "for we had rather relate that he was hanged at Tyburn (which may very probably be the case) than forfeit our integrity, or shock the faith of our reader."

This ironical attitude towards the reality of his creation was probably responsible in part for the main critical doubt which *Tom Jones* suggests. It is, in the main, a very true book, but it is by no means so clear that its truth has, to quote R. S. Crane, been "rendered" in terms of the novel. We do not get the impressive sense of Fielding's own moral qualities from his characters or their actions that we do from the heroic struggles for human betterment which he conducted as a magistrate under the most adverse personal circumstances, or even from *The Journal of a Voyage to Lisbon*; and if we analyse our impression from the novels alone it surely is evident that our residual impression of dignity and generosity comes mainly from the passages where Fielding is speaking in his own person. And this, surely, is the result of a technique which was deficient at least in the sense that it was unable to convey this larger moral significance through character and action alone, and could only supply it by means of a somewhat intrusive patterning of the plot and by direct editorial commentary. As Henry James put it: Tom Jones "has so much 'life' that it amounts, for the effect of comedy and application of satire, almost to his having a mind"; almost, but not quite, and so it was necessary that "his author—*he* handsomely possessed of a mind—[should have] such an amplitude of reflection for him and round him that we see him through the mellow air of Fielding's fine old moralism."

All this, of course, is not to say Fielding does not succeed: *Tom Jones* is surely entitled to the praise of an anonymous early admirer who called it "on the whole . . . the most lively book ever published." But it is a very personal and unrepeatable kind of success: Fielding's technique was too eclectic to become a permanent element in the tradition of the novel—*Tom Jones* is only part novel, and there is much else—picaresque tale, comic drama, occasional essay.

On the other hand, Fielding's departure from the canons of formal realism indicated very clearly the nature of the supreme problem which the new genre had to face. The tedious asseveration of literal authenticity in Defoe and to some extent in Richardson, tended to obscure the fact that, if the novel was to achieve equality of status with other genres it had to be brought into contact with the whole tradition of civilised values, and supplement its realism of presentation with a realism of assessment. To the excellent Mrs. Barbauld's query as to the grounds on which he considered Richardson to be a lesser writer than Shakespeare, Coleridge answered that "Richardson is *only* interesting." This is no doubt unfair as a total judgement on the author of *Clarissa,* but it indicates the likely limits of a realism of presentation: we shall be wholly immersed in the reality of the characters and their actions, but whether we shall be any wiser as a result is open to question.

Fielding brought to the genre something that is ultimately even more important than narrative technique—a responsible wisdom about human affairs which plays upon the deeds and the characters of his novels. His wisdom is not, perhaps, of the highest order; it is, like that of his beloved Lucian, a little inclined to be easygoing and on occasion opportunist. Nevertheless, at the end of *Tom Jones* we feel we have been exposed, not merely to an interesting narrative about imaginary persons, but to a stimulating wealth of suggestion and challenge on almost every topic of human interest. Not only so: the stimulation has come from a mind with a true grasp of human reality, never deceived or deceiving about himself, his characters or the human lot in general. In his effort to infuse the new genre with something of the Shakespearean virtues Fielding departed too far from formal realism to initiate a viable tradition, but his work serves as a perpetual reminder that if the new genre was to challenge older literary forms it had to find a way of conveying not only a convincing impression but a wise assessment of life, an assessment that could only come from taking a much wider view than Defoe or Richardson of the affairs of mankind.

So, although we must agree with the tenor of Johnson's watch simile, we must also add that it is unfair and misleading. Richardson, no doubt, takes us deeper into the inner workings of the human machine; but Fielding is surely entitled to retort that there are many other machines in nature besides the individual consciousness, and perhaps to express his surprised chagrin that Johnson should apparently have overlooked the fact that he was engaged in the exploration of a vaster and equally intricate mechanism, that of human society as a whole, a literary subject which was, incidentally, much more consonant than Richardson's with the classical outlook which he and Johnson shared.

"Fielding" in *Tom Jones*

Wayne C. Booth

Though the dramatized Fielding does serve to pull together many parts of *Tom Jones* that might otherwise seem disconnected, and though he serves dozens of other functions, from the standpoint of strict function he goes too far: much of his commentary relates to nothing but the reader and himself. If we really want to defend the book as art, we must somehow account for these "extraneous" elements. It is not difficult to do so, however, once we think of the effect of our intimacy on our attitude toward the book as a whole. If we read straight through all of the seemingly gratuitous appearances by the narrator, leaving out the story of Tom, we discover a running account of growing intimacy between the narrator and the reader, an account with a kind of plot of its own and a separate denouement. In the prefatory chapter to his final volume, the narrator makes this denouement explicit, suggesting a distinct interest in the "story" of his relationship with the reader. This interest certainly requires some explanation if we wish to claim that *Tom Jones* is a unified work of art and not half-novel, half-essay.

> We are now, reader, arrived at the last stage of our long journey. As we have, therefore, travelled together through so many pages, let us behave to one another like fellow-travellers in a stagecoach, who have passed several days in the company of each other; and who, notwithstanding any bickerings or little animosities which may have occurred on the road, generally

From *The Rhetoric of Fiction*. © 1961, 1983 by the University of Chicago. University of Chicago Press, 1983.

make all up at last, and mount, for the last time, into their vehicle with cheerfulness and good-humor.

The farewell goes on for several paragraphs, and at times the bantering tone of much of the work is entirely abandoned. "And now, my friend, I take this opportunity (as I shall have no other) of heartily wishing thee well. If I have been an entertaining companion to thee, I promise thee it is what I have desired. If in anything I have offended, it was really without any intention."

It may be extravagant to use the term "subplot" for the story of our relationship with this narrator. Certainly the narrator's "life" and Tom Jones's life are much less closely parallel than we expect in most plots and subplots. In *Lear,* Gloucester's fate parallels and reinforces Lear's. In *Tom Jones,* the "plot" of our relationship with Fielding-as-narrator has no similarity to the story of Tom. There is no complication, not even any sequence except for the gradually increasing familiarity and intimacy leading to farewell. And much of what we admire or enjoy in the narrator is in most respects quite different from what we like or enjoy in his hero.

Yet somehow a genuine harmony of the two dramatized elements is produced. It is from the narrator's norms that Tom departs when he gets himself into trouble, yet Tom is always in harmony with his most important norms. Not only does he reassure us constantly that Tom's heart is always in the right place, his presence reassures us of both the moral and the literary rightness of Tom's existence. As we move through the novel under his guidance, watching Tom sink to the depths, losing, as it appears, Allworthy's protection, Sophia's love, and his own shaky hold on decency, we experience for him what R. S. Crane has called the "comic analogue of fear." And our growing intimacy with Fielding's dramatic version of himself produces a kind of comic analogue of the true believer's reliance on a benign providence in real life. It is not just that he promises a happy ending. In a fictional world that offers no single character who is both wise and good—even Allworthy, though all worthy, is no model of perspicacity—the author is always there on his platform to remind us, through his wisdom and benevolence, of what human life ought to be and might be. What is more, his self-portrait is of a life enriched by a vast knowledge of literary culture and of a mind of great creative power—qualities which could never be so fully conveyed through simply exercising them without comment on the dramatic materials of Tom's story.

For the reader who becomes too much aware of the author's claim to superlative virtues, the effect may fail. He may seem merely to be posing. For the reader with his mind on the main business, however, the narrator becomes a rich and provocative chorus. It is his wisdom and learning and benevolence that permeate the world of the book, set its comic tone between the extremes of sentimental indulgence and scornful indignation, and in a sense redeem Tom's world of hypocrites and fools.

One can imagine, perhaps, a higher standard of virtue, wisdom, or learning than the narrator's. But for most of us he succeeds in being the highest possible in his world—and, at least for the nonce, in ours. He is not trying to write for any other world, but for *this* one he strikes the precise medium between too much and too little piety, benevolence, learning, and worldly wisdom. When he draws to the end of his farewell, then, at a time when we know we are to lose him, and uses terms which inevitably move us across the barrier to death itself, we find, lying beneath our amusement at his playful mode of farewell, something of the same feeling we have when we lose a close friend, a friend who has given us a gift which we can never repay. The gift he leaves—his book—is himself, precisely himself. The author has created this self as he has written the book. The book and the friend are one. "For however short the period may be of my own performances, they will most probably outlive their own infirm author, and the weakly productions of his abusive contemporaries." Was Fielding literally infirm as he wrote that sentence? It matters not in the least. It is not Fielding we care about, but the narrator created to speak in his name.

The Subversion of Forms

Martin Price

Fielding the novelist is consistent with Fielding the moralist. The novelist plays against forms just as much as the moralist. "Playing against" may need a word of explanation. The comic writer and the comic actor achieve some of their best effects by maintaining the traditional forms of heroism or morality—which provide their world with a stable and secure familiar meaning—but treating them with an excess of gravity, a curiously upsetting literalness, a pleasure in the dilemmas they pose. The high rhetoric invites this touch of fatuity by its very height, as I have tried to show in discussing the Augustan mock form; and the systematic embarrassment of the traditional view is the stuff of comedy. In *The Tragedy of Tragedies* Fielding subverted forms with a high-spirited extravagance, but the forms he subverted were extremely susceptible to this treatment. The same may be said of *Shamela,* where he reduces Richardson's Pamela to a trollop with a simpleminded delight in her cunning. On one level or another this subversion of forms runs through Fielding's work; even when it is not used primarily as a comic technique, it represents a saving skepticism, a readiness to examine every possible imposture, even those that his heroes assume.

Let me illustrate. In *Jonathan Wild* the burden of the irony is carried by the villainy of Wild and his rapacious colleagues (as well as their counterparts in the high life of court). But once the innocent Heartfrees escape Wild's exploitation and are reunited with great joy, Mrs. Heartfree

From *To the Palace of Wisdom: Studies in Order and Energy from Dryden to Blake.* © 1964 by Martin Price. Southern Illinois University Press, 1964.

takes up her astonishing recital of her adventures. Her account is a parody of romance literature, but it also reveals the awakened vanity of a simple woman who has discovered her power over men. We can perhaps acquit her of deliberately torturing her husband with protracted accounts of attempts upon her virtue, but she tends to dwell on the compliments she has received.

> "If I mistake not, I was interrupted just as I was beginning to repeat some of the compliments made me by the hermit." "Just as you had finished them, I believe, madam," said the justice. "Very well, sir," said she; "I am sure I have no pleasure in the repetition. He concluded then with telling me, though I was in his eyes the most charming woman in the world, and might tempt a saint to abandon the ways of holiness, yet my beauty inspired him."

And she goes on, unsparingly, apparently anxious to relive those moments of unfamiliar glory.

Something like this occurs in *Amelia* when Mrs. Atkinson tells her story to Amelia. Having raised her listener to a high pitch of curiosity, Mrs. Atkinson begins the long torture of delay and apology, pleased with her power over her audience, sure of the appeal of her subject. The tale reveals a good deal of pettiness in the teller, and the flood of emotions that are released demands draughts of cordial, glasses of water, and at least one violent convulsion fit that lasts "the usual time."

This constant ironic reservation and readiness to overthrow whatever has grown suspect through hardening into formality link Fielding with some of our contemporary novelists. Kingsley Amis has spoken of his humor as "closer to our own than that of any writer before the present century," and has found "a Fielding revival" in the rejection by contemporaries of "the novel of consistent tone, moving through a recognized and restricted cycle of emotional keys." These novelists are comparable to Fielding in their attempt "to combine the violent and the absurd, the grotesque and the romantic, the farcical and the horrific within a single novel." Amis overlooks the appeal of Fielding to writers like Stendhal and Gide, who achieved in considerable measure what the postwar English novel has attempted. But his point is important, and it is the kind of critical view that deserves the closest attention because it comes out of the problems of new literary creation.

The kind of writing that most closely resembles Fielding's today is the comic picaresque novel, like Amis's own *Lucky Jim,* in which the hero makes up in honesty for what he lacks in respectability. His inability to live as prudently as others who are less honest and simply less alive produces a series of farcical scrapes. These are often painful, but they are so extravagantly elaborate and so ingeniously invented that our sympathy is displaced into laughter. The laughter is not without its edge—Lucky Jim's desperate efforts to save appearances are a tribute to the power of the conventions he has to live by in order to live at all. But the picaresque hero is at once a moral critic (like the satirist posing as *naïf* or *ingénu*), a careless innocent, and—in his comic resilience—a man saved by luck. Picaresque heroes are necessary whenever we wish to celebrate those virtues that cannot be—or simply haven't been—embodied in our morality. These heroes may be socially mobile men in an age of outgrown establishments, or they may be champions of values that society, by its very organization, necessarily represses. The resilience and survival of the picaresque hero is a survival of the values he stands for, values too closely involved with action to be put to sleep in Avalon. They must be seen in their readiness and their openness, and the picaresque work often concludes with the arc of a new gesture about to be made.

Yet it is not the picaresque hero alone that gives Fielding's novels their distinctive note, but the combination of naïve hero and sophisticated narrator. The fluid shifts of tone that we see in recent picaresque novels are produced by heroes (usually narrators as well) who are open to each new experience, variable and unpredictable, often self-mocking. In these novels the reader is left without a clear guide; he follows along as he can, prepared only for surprise. But in Fielding's novels the case is different. Tom Jones may be spontaneous and improvident, but he surprises himself more than he does the reader. We see him through the narrator's commentary, in a series of events that are clearly calculated and tellingly repetitive—so that he becomes a comic figure fixed in a limited pattern of response. We count on Tom's goodness and on his carelessness. It is the novelist, instead, who engages our curiosity. How will he bring it all off? How will he extricate his hero and, even more, his values? The novelist's relationship with the reader—itself, as Wayne Booth has suggested, a subplot in the novel—is carefully modulated between doubt and trust, ironic aloofness and warm solidarity. The characters, hero and all, play out their roles within the space that Fielding creates and encloses in his relationship with the reader.

What is this relationship? Here we meet the problem we find in all Augustan irony. Ultimately, behind the work we see the historical author, the real personality behind the mask. In some cases, like Pope's late satires, where the author has become a public figure, our recognition of his actual traits may be essential. But generally before we come at that figure, we have the mask itself to meet. The Fielding who appears in his novels is, like Swift and Pope, a shifting series of personae; he is engaged in a constant dance of ironic postures. Behind them we may recognize a personality we can trust and accept, but we know him through his performance.

Let us consider a single instance of this. In the opening chapter of *Joseph Andrews* the author praises the power of example as opposed to mere precept: "A good man . . . is a standing lesson to all his acquaintance, and of far greater use in that narrow circle than a good book." This we can take on trust: "a standing lesson" is a little chilling and might seem an invitation to self-righteousness, but it need not trouble us. Fielding goes on, then, to consider the problem of making such a lesson available to the world at large, beyond the small circle of a good man's personal acquaintance; it is the writer who can achieve this end, and "by communicating such valuable patterns to the world, he may perhaps do a more extensive service to mankind, than the person whose life originally afforded the pattern." Again, this is plausible enough (Pope has done more for mankind than the Man of Ross), but it is disconcerting: the good man is now opposed to the writer of his history, and heroic goodness is made a less "extensive service to mankind" than the art of the biographer. We seem to be confusing values, and a phrase like "service to mankind" carries the seeds of the confusion. What, we ask, would the biographer have to represent without the "standing lesson" itself? The outside—the representation, the biography or legend—seems to be supplanting the active goodness that is so rare.

The subversion becomes clear as we move on to some examples of this "service to mankind": "John the Great, who, by his brave and heroic actions against men of large and athletic bodies, obtained the glorious appellation of the Giant-Killer." The nursery tales and romances are solemnly offered as the means by which "the reader is almost as much improved as entertained." This may be true; nursery tales do instill moral awareness. But the pompous claims begin to strike a false note.

This false note is now carried over to the two works Fielding offers as an "admirable pattern of the amiable"—Colley Cibber's *Apology* and Richardson's *Pamela*. All the implicit self-advertising of the "biographer or historian" is now lightly dropped on the shoulders of Richardson, who pretended to be working "from authentic papers and records." And Colley Cibber embodies the complete subversion of the relationship of "standing lesson" and "biographer." He is both at once, and "is by many thought to have lived such a life only in order to write it." The point of all this is that appearance and pretension have swallowed up the goodness they claim to serve, and Fielding has set the satirical keynote for his novel in the opening paragraphs.

Fielding is addressing his reader at two levels. He is speaking to the perceptive and good-natured man, but he is constantly teasing him with the possibility that he is not up to this candor. Readers, like other men, are conventional, snobbish, hypocritical; and, in any case, the morality of Fielding's novels is designed to unsettle accepted attitudes. If the reader is to achieve the flexibility and discrimination that Fielding's morality demands, he must be teased into a full exercise of his wits. Just as Fielding so often maintains an ironic courtesy toward his characters and hesitates over which motive to ascribe to them (meanwhile, of course, exposing the worst), so he is often embarrassingly tactful to his readers. His tact is the sort that makes its victim aware of how tenderly he must be treated, or, in other words, how little he can be trusted. The man who deserves to be trusted needs no tact; the banter of friends can be free and playful, and the author's irony will then only confirm his solidarity with the reader. But, in the process, there are few readers whose feelings are not tested and whose wit is not sharpened.

The structure of Fielding's major novels is a distinctive combination of elements. His comic plots are elaborate and contrived, but within them there is room for the casualness of picaresque incident; they have the artificiality of stage comedy and the leisurely looseness of a more realistic form. His heroes engage our feelings, surely, but they do not have enough consciousness to allow us to inhabit their minds very long or live there very fully. They do not stretch our awareness or offer the sense of limitlessness our own experience does. They have the measure of reality we confer upon many childhood memories: we can feel ourselves back into that simpler mind and know what it was like, but we cannot suppress our sense of what was not yet there. Tom Jones has traditionally been taken as a somewhat autobiographical character. Whether or not he was in fact, the book presents the effect of the mature author contemplating himself when younger—somewhat more equably than Byron does in *Don Juan*—with detachment but with warmth.

The presence of the author is an element that affects all the rest. He presents us with a microcosm to be contemplated, puzzled over, studied. As he puts it in *Tom Jones*, "This work may . . . be considered as a great creation of our own; and for a little reptile of a critic to presume to find fault with any of its parts, without knowing the manner in which the whole is connected . . . is a most presumptuous absurdity." This is a defense of the literary structure, but Fielding's deliberate echo of Pope's *Essay on Man* is telling: he points in the next paragraph to the "nice distinctions"—Pope calls them gradations—"between two persons activated by the same vice or folly as another." Fielding's novel is a world to be studied as God's creation is studied in the *Essay on Man,* and his diction throughout the book creates categories of discursive thought. We are made to apprehend Fielding's world conceptually. This device is often playful; the concepts are too inclusive to do more than mock the sorry things they denote. But we are always told as well as shown, or told as we are shown. Fielding keeps us constantly aware of the problem we have in coming to terms with a fluid world and an elusive spontaneous goodness by means of the concepts our minds have to make do with. Significantly, Fielding's minor characters talk a great deal; and they reveal in the process the treacherous nature of conceptual language.

Not only the language, but the arrangement of parts in Fielding's novels has a discursive form. Again and again characters are paired off to present false extremes. Or a cast of characters is led past Tom's bedside (as he recovers from the injury he sustained in rescuing Sophia) to cheer him or berate him, to exhibit different shades of love, benevolence, malice, or vindictiveness. Or all the characters execute a dance of attitudes around a single concept—love in *Tom Jones,* charity in *Joseph Andrews.* Characters are created to fill out a moral spectrum, and each gains from the presence of the rest: "the follies of either rank do in reality illustrate each other," as Fielding tells us. We are teased and challenged once more by the problem of arranging these characters. Where shall we place Squire Western in any scale that runs from Allworthy to Blifil? But all these discursive effects would have little interest if they were not constantly played off against the narrative movement and our sympathies with the characters. Fielding is neither essayist nor realistic novelist, nor both in turn. He is rather both at once and therefore something different from either.

In such novels as Fielding writes, neither characters nor action can be allowed to escape the author's control. Fielding controls his characters by limiting them. In general, his heroes have more energy than reflectiveness, although all have their moments of dignified eloquence. The villains, in turn, are so transparent (but not to men like Allworthy) and so compulsive that we are left with an impression of moral shallowness more than depravity. There are bullies and braggarts, misers and hypocrites, but no one to say, "Evil, be thou my good." These characters are all dependent upon the social forms that give them a guise of respectability, and the forms—or dogmas or twisted meanings—become as responsible as the people who use them. Fielding brings this out through his symmetrical arrangements. He boasts, for example, of his description of "the different operations of this passion of love in the gentle and cultivated mind of the Lady Booby, from those which it effected in the less polished and coarser disposition of Mrs. Slipslop." Again in book 2 of *Tom Jones* he gives us "scenes of matrimonial felicity in different degrees of life." Here Mrs. Partridge's uncontrolled suspicions of her husband's relations with Jenny Jones produce Punch-and-Judy farce, while the hatred of Captain Blifil and his wife has a savage intensity that is possible only with a more refined etiquette. The Blifils' marriage is summed up in the widow's mourning:

> [She] conducted herself through the whole season in which grief is to make its appearance on the outside of the body with the strictest regard to all the rules of custom and decency, suiting the alterations of her countenance to the several alterations of her habit: for as this changed from weeds to black, from black to gray, from gray to white, so did her countenance change from dismal to sorrowful, from sorrowful to sad, and from sad to serious, till the day came in which she was allowed to return to her former serenity.

The word "allowed," ironic as it is, reminds us that, while the depth of malice may be directly proportionate to the complexity of forms, the forms themselves exercise a tyranny over the man who lives by them. We see something much like this in Restoration comedy; the case of Fainall in *The Way of the World* comes to mind, and the way in which Mirabell seizes the forms and turns them to a better purpose. Fielding's heroes do not attempt what Mirabell so handsomely carries off—or rather they bring new difficulties upon themselves when they do attempt it. Tom's proposal of marriage to Lady Bellaston succeeds in freeing him of a demanding mistress, but it rebounds against him when Sophia learns of it. Amelia sends Mrs. Atkinson to the masquerade in her place and eludes her would-be seducer, but she gives Mrs. Atkinson's indiscretion occasion to create new difficulties.

Another severe limitation Fielding places upon his characters is the importance that rumor and gossip play in determining their fate. We see Tom pursued along the road by malicious reports; Tom and Sophia kept at odds by the petty jealousy of their servants, Partridge and Honour. (Only rarely does the reverse work out, as when Tom's kindness to Anderson, the desperate highwayman, becomes known to Mrs. Miller and ultimately to Allworthy.) What gives Fielding's world its peculiar quality is that so much happens with so little design. There is a great deal of triviality—the snobbery of a Mrs. Graveairs, the weak swagger of a Beau Didapper, the autumnal lust of Mrs. Slipslop—some of it disarmingly grotesque, too mechanically incongruous to seem very menacing, but all of it building up through a crisscross of coincidence and a steady accumulation to formidable proportions. When Jack Nightingale seduces Nancy Miller, Tom must spell out to Nightingale the meaning of what he has done: "I do not imagine you have laid a regular premeditated scheme for the destruction of the quiet of a poor little creature, or have even foreseen the consequence: for I am sure thou art a very good-natured fellow, and such a one can never be guilty of a cruelty of that kind; but at the same time you have pleased your vanity, without considering that this poor girl was made a sacrifice to it."

Fielding's interest, then, lies less in the moral struggles within characters than in the ways in which selfishness finds refuge in forms. Lady Booby and Black George are both shown in formal deliberation, balancing alternatives with all the scruples of a high tragic character; but the formal deliberation also provides a comfortable disguise—from themselves—of the meanness of their motives. Fielding has taken over from Mandeville the close study of the way in which social forms are learned. His delightful account of the young girl's schooling in coquetry derives from The Fable of the Bees and turns all Mandeville's cruel insights upon Richardson's Pamela as well as Lady Booby. Fielding can use Mandeville's reductive analysis of motives to good purpose so long as he is treating vanity and folly; it is Mandeville's similar account of the origin of moral virtue that he indignantly rejects.

Like Mandeville, Fielding has a detached appreciation of the artistry of our vanities and passions, particularly as they make use of social forms. One example will serve. Squire Western's sister is a woman of shallow vanity, tall, ugly, unloved, who has found her compensations not in prudery, like Bridget Allworthy, but in a studious devotion to the fashionable world. She has "acquired all that knowledge which the said world usually communicates; and was a perfect mistress of manners, customs, ceremonies, and fashions." She has studied her plays and romances, her historical memoirs and political pamphlets; she has mastered "the doctrine of Amour" and the latest gossip—"a knowledge which she the more easily attained, as her pursuit of it was never diverted by any affairs of her own." It is a wonderful picture of an empty woman feeding upon externalities and vicarious excitement. And, of course, she speaks a dreadful gibberish of court lingo, diplomatic jargon, and military terms. The gibberish gives away her innocent incomprehension of all she imagines she knows, even as her pride in devious subtlety makes her parrot the cynicism of the town. When Squire Western remarks, "Allworthy is a queer b—ch, and money hath no effect o' un," she can reply, "Do you think Allworthy hath more contempt for money than any other man because he professes more? Such credulity would better become one of us weak women, than that wise sex which Heaven hath formed for politicians." She is, of course, the most credulous of creatures herself. But all her affection for her brother and niece, all her fundamental goodness ("a very extraordinary good and sweet disposition") can produce, under the influence of fashionable forms upon her vanity, is the astonishing advice that Sophia marry Blifil so that she may have Tom safely as a lover.

Such innocent depravity as Mrs. Western's—and it is not much different from Jack Nightingale's or Lord Fellamar's—shows the diffusion of responsibility Fielding creates in his world. Actions follow from small vanities as often as from deliberate evil. They may be the product of a chance meeting of characters who are in themselves ineffectual but become imposing in combination. Thus, when Sophia and Tom almost meet at Upton, they are kept apart by a series of accidents—yet in retrospect all that happens follows from the nature of the participants. Sophia's maid, Honour, exhibits all her pretensions in the inn kitchen as she loftily allows Partridge, who has come with Tom, to remain: "you look somewhat like a gentleman, and may sit still if you please: I don't desire to disturb anybody but mob." When Honour is sent by Sophia to call Tom, Partridge struts in turn: "One woman is enough at once for a reasonable man." His manner enrages Honour, who at once reports Tom's infidelity to Sophia and gives it as ugly a turn as possible. To make matters worse, Susan the chambermaid can relay Partridge's boasts "that your ladyship was dying for love of the young squire, and that he was going to the wars to get rid of you." This formidable array of pettiness provides a constant store of motives Fielding can bring into play with the slightest twist of coincidence. The result is that the coincidences that entrap the central characters seem only special cases of the prevailing conditions that surround them. This enables Fielding to use the most flagrant artifice without our losing touch with a plausible social reality.

Fielding's subversion of forms, at work throughout his novels, becomes most apparent in his comic resolutions, which can still outrage moralistic critics by their disdain for the full consequences of the heroes' frailties. Yet the artifice that resolves the near-catastrophe is the same as the artifice that creates it. Fielding weaves together blind and confused motives to bring his heroes to the brink of disasters they hardly merit. And the excess of these disasters makes them ludicrous, morally as well as dramatically. Fielding sharpens this by inventing, in both *Joseph Andrews* and *Tom Jones,* a travesty of the prototypical tragic nemesis, the dark mystery of unknowing incest. His point is that these terrors are not for such heroes as these; the incursion of the terrible into this world of limited consciousness and limited consequences is brilliantly unreal.

When Joseph and Fanny learn that they are apparently brother and sister, Fielding crowds the discovery scene with noisy emotion that suggests panic in a barnyard when a fox has entered. Joseph and Fanny grow faint and pallid, but little Dicky Adams roars and Parson Adams falls to his knees to ejaculate many thanksgivings. And Adams himself is to undergo, in the night farce of mistaken bedrooms, the test of being discovered by Joseph naked in bed with Fanny ("Hath he offered any rudeness to you?" Joseph asks in a rage). The novel never relaxes long enough to take the threat of incest seriously or to make more than ridiculous the resolutions with which it is met. Adams's advice is feeble enough, and it is followed by the vow of Joseph and Fanny of "perpetual celibacy." They plan, poor fools, "to live together all their days, and indulge a Platonic friendship for each other."

In *Tom Jones,* once the seeming fact that Tom has slept with his mother is revealed, we have tragic postures and a near-tragic speech: "But why do I blame Fortune? I am myself the cause of all my misery." But at this point the author intrudes to remind us how artfully he had managed the ninth book to prevent Partridge from meeting Mrs. Waters there. We are reminded not only of the fictionality of character and event, but of the absurdly intensified causality Fielding has created: "Instances of this kind we may frequently observe in life, where the greatest events are produced by a nice train of little circumstances; and more than one example of this may be discovered by the accurate eye, in this our history." Once more in *Amelia,* when the bailiff apprehends Booth outside Miss Matthew's lodgings just before he can return to Amelia, our attention is directed to the artifice that runs through all these novels and tightens causality to the point where it verges on the farcical:

> There is no exercise of the mind of a sensible reader more
> pleasant than tracing the several small and almost impercep-
> tible links in every chain of events by which all the great ac-
> tions of the world are produced.

We are made securely aware of the novelist in control, and we recognize
that the terrible has been prepared as deftly and artificially as it will be
overturned.

Is this cheating moral seriousness? Fielding has so arranged matters
that there is no Thwackum-like punitive nemesis; he has subverted the
form in which men have traditionally embodied their sense of guilt: their
fear of the price that greatness must exact, their sense of the exposure to
irretrievable error that comes of each new assertion of power or will.
Tom has approached a tragic role throughout the last part as he assumes
responsibility at each turn for what he has done. So here: "I am myself
the cause of all my misery." And we can admire this, but we recognize
the disproportion between the act and its consequences. Only a sinister
deity would design such punishment, the kind of deity who invites pros-
tration or defiance rather than trust. The fact that the tragic discovery is
traditional does not, in short, make it appropriate; Fielding shrugs off the
great tragic forms with a Christian cheerfulness. Dr. Harrison, when he
writes to Booth and Amelia about their loss of her mother's fortune,
congratulates them upon their happiness in each other. "A superstitious
heathen," he goes on, "would have dreaded the malice of Nemesis in
your situation; but as I am a Christian, I shall venture to add another
circumstance to your felicity . . . that you have . . . a faithful and zealous
friend."

The result has its own kind of moral seriousness. Fielding insists
upon the weight of folly and triviality that impedes the best and worst
intentions. In the preface to his sister's *David Simple,* Fielding speaks of
"the mazes, windings, and labyrinths, which perplex the heart of man
to such a degree that he is himself often incapable of seeing through
them." In his own novels, his typical method is to place heroes of transparent and spontaneous goodness (they may have innocent follies and
affectations, like Adams) amidst the mazes and windings of others' selfishness. These heroes need not succeed, and they come to recognize this
fact; but they need not fail, either, in a world where evil often becomes
self-defeating and Fortune seems to rule. Fortune is the name we give to
the impenetrable intricacy of those "nice trains of little causes" or "small

and almost imperceptible links in every chain of events." The links are, in most cases, the trivial obsessions of others, the inevitable accidents of countless jostling egos.

Fielding can reward his heroes because they do not seek a reward. He wishes to free our faith in Order, as Pope does, from any simple-minded expectation that goodness will find its reward on earth. The only reward it can find there is that it pays to itself: the pleasure it finds in doing good and in sustaining its integrity. Beyond that it seeks nothing, and, in seeking nothing, it has earned the reward the author confers. The comic resolutions are not devices for saving these heroes from facing moral consequences but rewards for their having done so. That the reward is externalized and paid in solid pudding rather than praise need not alter the point. That, too, is a way of reminding us that the malignant Fortune that hounds these characters and the comic providence that extricates them are only two aspects of the author himself, as they are of a benevolent deity. Those characters who can act as if there were such a God of course find Him:

> Earth smiles around, with boundless bounty blest,
> And Heaven beholds its image in his breast.
> (*Essay on Man,* 4.371–72)

Fielding the Novelist:
The Lucianic Satirist

Ronald Paulson

Fielding's growing interest in motive shows how far he has gone beyond the self-imposed limits of the satirist. As a satirist he is overwhelmingly interested in actions, and his aim is to distinguish the good from the evil—thus he places commentators around actions in his earlier works so that both can be readily understood. In *Joseph Andrews* he shows that by analyzing the action itself, one can see through the individual's professions. Pamela says she wants to escape from Mr. B., but if her reactions are examined by themselves it becomes obvious that she really does not. Even at the outset, action with Fielding is a way of dramatizing motive. But inevitably Fielding must also ask himself: what of those undeniably pious actions such as Pamela's resisting Mr. B.'s lecherous advances and fleeing at his approach? Here the action by itself cannot be interpreted, he would argue, without reference to Pamela's motives. How much is it her virtue of chastity and how much her mercenary desire to substitute the role of wife for the less profitable one of mistress?

Richardson is interested in Pamela's professions and actions; Fielding, in her motives. Richardson claims that her professions and actions tell us her motives; Fielding suspects a radical discrepancy. The satirist ordinarily makes much the same claim as does Richardson (he admits that motives are slippery and thus relies only on concrete examples of conduct), but he is never accused of hypocrisy because he keeps an external and firm control on his characters. By contrast, Fielding's concern

From *Satire and the Novel in Eighteenth-Century England.* © 1967 by Yale University. Yale University Press, 1967.

with motives, which begins to be noticeable in *Joseph Andrews,* is distinctly un-Augustan; there is never a question of a discrepancy between an action and a motive in Swift's satire, only between words and motives or actions. But in the Good Samaritan scene of *Joseph Andrews* character is judged as much through motive as action: the lawyer would take Joseph into the coach, but for the wrong reason (he is afraid, being among the last people in Joseph's company, that he will be called to account for his death). Betty the chambermaid is kind to Joseph but her motive is at least partly sexual attraction. Again, landladies of inns refuse Joseph service because they think him a peasant, and other equally bad landladies lavish service on him thinking him a lord.

Charity, as it often appears in *Joseph Andrews,* is an objective action and so far does not depart from the criteria of the Augustan satirists. But the Latitudinarians and, with them, Fielding tended to divorce the inner motive from the outer expression, or character from conduct. While agreeing that objectively a good action must be judged by its good effect on other people, they claimed that the only real criterion was the motive from which the action sprang. As Archbishop Tillotson, the first Latitudinarian Archbishop of Canterbury, put it: if we are good "only to serve our temporal interest, though the actions we do be never so good, yet all the virtue and reward of them is lost, by the mean end and design which we aim at in the doing of them." In the same way, though an action directed by a good motive goes astray, it is nevertheless a good action. The motive of love or charity—already encountered in the Heartfrees as foils to Jonathan Wild—makes it good. Parson Adams, although he stresses works ("What signifies knowing your duty, if you do not perform it?"), is often prevented from carrying them out, despite his good intentions. When he offers the Catholic priest money, he finds he has none to give, and when he tries to comfort Joseph over the loss of Fanny, he in fact increases Joseph's grief. Although objectified in Adams's attempt to help the priest, and to some extent censured in the treatment of Joseph, the inwardness toward which Fielding is pointing can become in certain instances very difficult to prove; moreover, it is not unrelated to the Quaker's inner light and the Puritan's conscience, both more concerned with private salvation than public welfare and both venerable targets of the Augustan satirists. Fielding's Latitudinarian heritage may be thought to run counter to his satiric intention much as Richardson's own sense of objective reality does to his moral aim.

Though *Pamela* derives from a Puritan and middle-class sensibility, it expresses a certainty in the rightness of form, convention, and tradition

that is also Augustan (with the radical exception of the democratic over-
tones of the servant girl's marriage to her master, which is wholly middle
class). As Bernard Kreissman has noticed, "Being blind to the 'inwardness' of virtue, Richardson could not conceive a virtuous character like
Parson Adams, who was outwardly hot-tempered, eccentric, and loud."
Neither could Swift and Pope. While they attack the ridiculous behavior
in which vanity manifests itself, Fielding attacks the invisible motives in
apparently proper behavior. This amounts, finally, to an attack on the
reality beneath the card-game of Augustan form, which Pope smiles at
in *The Rape of the Lock* but accepts as part of the world of order that
extends upward to marriage, the state, and the church.

It is perhaps ironic that with opposed intentions Fielding and Richardson have, in one respect, come up with the result intended by the
other. Fielding, intending to show the importance of character over actual
conduct, uses the Augustan's external techniques of irony and authorial
omniscience; he has to explain motives objectively, make them as schematic and visible as physical actions. On the other hand, Richardson,
concerned with the forms of virtue, conveys a powerful sense of his
characters' inner being. It is equally significant that Fielding attacked
Richardson less for breaking with the old, traditional forms (as Swift,
following from his *Tale of a Tub*, would have done) than for espousing a
morality that maintained the primacy of appearances and forms over
subjective character. Fielding tries to connect his form with the past, and
a classical Odysseus or Aeneas, a biblical Joseph or Abraham, often stands
behind his characters as a yardstick of value. But the ancient who influ-
enced him most was neither Horace nor Juvenal, but the cynical Lucian,
who believed that man's mind is for seeing through frauds and lies imposed on us by our fathers and grandfathers, by judges and lawyers,
philosophers and priests.

More than any of the other great classical satirists, Lucian is rheto-
rician first and moralist second, and his constant striving for surprise
sometimes suggests that the effect is achieved for its own sake. He depends on the surprise of exposure, on making the apparently indefensible
defensible, the apparently guilty innocent, the apparently noble ignoble.
Perhaps partly for this reason, Lucian has no strong bias to a particular
good as Juvenal does and no desire to map a subtle spiritual course for
the reader as Horace does. His aim is double—to expose the real, however
deep he must go under the illusions man weaves for himself; and to
discomfit his reader, shake up his cherished values and disrupt his orthodoxy. Lucian is the epitome of the satirist who writes at what he regards

a time of extreme stodginess and reaction, when values have become standardized and rigid.

The typical Lucianic fiction has a markedly mobile protagonist asking questions: he travels over the earth, or up to Olympus to question the gods, or down to Hades to question the dead—always probing appearances, idealization, myth, and custom. He is very different from the Horatian observer, solidly within society looking out, or the Juvenalian, a last fragment of the true society that has been isolated or expelled. He is not even necessarily a good man since his value is only as disrupter of orthodox and questioner of long-held assumptions. In the *Dialogues of the Dead,* Diogenes, whom Lucian elsewhere attacks as merely another false philosopher, acts as a disruptive agent whose questioning, probing, and railing serve a useful corrective function.

Lucianic satire works for Fielding in two areas—in the character of Tom and in the commentator's point of view. Tom, like Diogenes or Rabelais's Panurge, represents an excess that must at intervals be placed in relation to other values, and his satiric function is split between being a touchstone to test other characters and a corrective to expose their formalism. These two roles, passive and active, explain Tom insofar as he carries the traces of a rhetorical device. The second is clearly related to the Panurgic life-force. At a time when the Augustan reaction against freedom and individualism had perhaps gone too far, Fielding places his emphasis on a counter-reaction in favor of breaking stereotypes and outworn categories, espousing the value of feeling as well as form, instinct as well as reason. Hypocrisy, for example, was a vice usually attacked from the security of a conservative, decorous society; the subject was the man who pretended to be part of society but was in fact an outsider. Fielding, however, uses Tom to attack the hypocrite from a position virtually outside society, from which, momentarily at least, both the virtues the hypocrite pretends to and his pretense appear less real and true than the natural feeling of a Tom Jones.

Shaftesbury's doctrine of ridicule as a test of truth probably served as the mediator between Lucian's cheerful cynicism and Fielding's adaptation of disruptive satire as one strain of *Tom Jones*. Running through the novel is the belief (though qualified by other, sometimes contrary, doubts) that man, like all creation, is basically good and can only be corrupted by externals—education, institutions, and customs. Thus, if the satirist can bring ridicule to play, these will be cleared away. In general, as was evident in the case of Fielding's early villains, fashion clogs the natural wellsprings of good nature in man; the false ideal of the "great man" withered the good nature in him and made him a one-sided humor-character. This semi-Pelagian view of man, which may have contributed something to the ambiguity of Fielding's early villains, is exactly the opposite of the Augustan satirist's view. Swift would say that men are all born with feeble intellect and moral sense, but the best of men realize their limitations and seek the guidance of church and tradition. Institutions are necessary to curb man's dangerous proclivities. Fielding, how-ever, tends to suggest in *Tom Jones* that they may corrupt the good-natured man.

Forms for Fielding, however, are usually carefully defined as those things which are essentially illusory—opinions, habits, rumors, and the like. Besides giving Fielding a philosophical rationale for Lucianic satire, Shaftesbury gave him the groundwork for a spectrum of good and evil in which nothing is finally evil except various kinds of misunderstanding; in short, a metaphysical basis for a novel of manners in which social patterns of behavior could be contrasted with natural inclinations. In *Tom Jones,* moreover, the Shaftesburyian platonism extends to the very limits of Tom's world and accounts for such questionable events as the sudden dissipation of the threatened catastrophe followed by the happy ending. Tom, having lost Sophia, lying in the shadow of Tyburn, and believing that he has committed incest, seems to be doomed. But Fielding shows that this is all the world of appearances with which Tom has been clash-ing from the beginning: appearance can breed only appearance, and the reality was the bread Tom cast upon the waters in his acts of benevolence to Mrs. Miller and others. Tom has on his side such staunch friends as Mrs. Miller, while Blifil's plot depends on those qualities of form listed above—opinion, rumor, and such supporters as Dowling. Toward the end of *Tom Jones* letters begin to arrive at the right time, as do people, and Blifil's shoddy creation, which all along has been shaky and doomed, begins to come tumbling down, exactly according to Shaftesbury's prophecy, and exactly like Achitophel's at the end of Dryden's satire. All that separates this happy ending from the Augustan assumptions is that evil leaves no marks, no Adams, Eves, or Absaloms ruined along the way, and so it is less a perversion of the real than an excrescence on it.

But forms also include qualities, indeed institutions, that are less illusory and closer to the values defended by the Augustans; and Tom, being a corrective in the tradition of Lucian and Rabelais, does not always distinguish real from illusory forms when his feeling comes into play. His "good nature," the positive part of Fielding's doctrine, is the equiv-alent of the burst of energy that characterized the disruptive activity of

Diogenes or Panurge and the wide-ranging alternative to the narrow morality of sexual chastity (the single choice between marriage and infamy) of Richardson's world. Again following the Latitudinarians and Shaftesbury, Fielding sometimes suggests that moral judgment is based less on intellection than on feeling, which is connected, of course, with the belief that man is basically good. "Good breeding" is the social quality in Fielding's system—doing to others that which you would like them to do to you. But at the bottom of "good breeding" is "good nature," that innate, almost inner-light quality. The criterion for one's actions is charity, or "good breeding," and the person with abundant "good nature" will always act from a charitable motive in a given situation. He will feel a veritable and "glorious lust of doing good."

A modern in the armor of the ancients, Fielding seems to have carried with him both the need of authority and confidence in intuition. Authority is transmuted in *Tom Jones* into the commonsense quality called prudence, which should be used to check even the best of passions—but which may be very unpleasant by itself. Thus Tom, as a character, is shown to be "mixed" in a more radical sense than Joseph and Parson Adams. His exuberance sometimes ends in pain to others as well as himself and is an extension of the physically vigorous young man, not, as with Adams, a contradiction of the spiritual. Perhaps closer to Adams than to Joseph, Tom is persecuted by a wicked society but deserves his persecution just enough to benefit from it and so become a more balanced person at the end than he was at the beginning. Tom's quixotic aberration is his "good nature," his "good breeding," which makes him go to the extreme of giving his body to young or old ladies out of a deep inner compulsion to generosity and love. And so while his good nature may be interpreted on one side as the proper corrective to Thwackum and Blifil, on the other it may be called momentary self-indulgence. Fielding, however, interprets it according to Quixote: Tom fastens his attention on one aspect of an object and makes it into the whole: just as the whirling blades of a windmill became the flailing arms of a giant for Quixote, so the white breasts of Mrs. Waters or the generosity of Lady Bellaston or the appearance of youth and availability in Molly lead Tom to break with both prudence and moral laws. He is as oblivious to appearances as Quixote: Fielding keeps emphasizing this, and the need for prudence, throughout the novel, until at the end we are told that Tom has reached a balance between feeling (his quixotic madness) and form.

It is not, however, Tom Jones—the corrective or the mixed character—but Fielding's commentator-narrator who best demonstrates the use of Lucianic satire. He is the observer and questioner who probes past appearances, dropping the arras that conceals Square, and exploring the mixed quality of experience. The commentator's most potent tool is once again his irony, but now it is a more complex instrument used to question rather than affirm.

In *Joseph Andrews* the irony directed at the lecherous Lady Booby serves as both denigration and an indication of her own false picture of herself—a rhetorical and a psychological effect. But there is perhaps a third effect, which William Empson characterizes when he says that Fielding "seems to leave room for the ideas he laughs at." In some sense Lady Booby really is, as she claims, heroically battling her passions, just as Quixote's illusions in some sense contain truth. While this is a very slight impression as concerns Lady Booby, it does explain something about our reaction to Parson Adams, who *is* both wise (as he thinks) and foolish. In *Tom Jones* Empson finds what he calls "double irony" to be a controlling principle. This might be called "both/and" irony, because it gives some credence to both "the contrary" and "what one means," or to the praise and the blame. When Fielding says that Black George, who has just stolen Tom's money, really does love Tom, he is saying a number of different things—that Black George has persuaded himself by rationalization that he loves Tom, but also that there is a sense in which Black George really does love him, even if at the moment he loves money more. While single irony implies the author's grasp of all circumstances and eventualities, with the proper subordination of the false to the true, double irony suggests a greater tolerance, a delicate poise, or mere uncertainty. The effect is close to the unsubordinated *copia* of Richardsonian realism and suggests an attempt to achieve "realism of presentation" as well as "realism of assessment."

Our study of *Joseph Andrews* has shown that Fielding was not impervious to the success of kinds of realism other than his own. In *Tom Jones* the Richardsonian signs can be recognized at once—more facts, more information about everything, more extenuating circumstances recorded, and more different motives and attitudes to choose from, all creating a general plenitude. The irony helps to generate this impression; instead of a single statement (such as the one about Lady Booby's passion) Fielding gives two or more possibilities, some very plausible. Here are Mrs. Wilkins's reasons for obeying Squire Allworthy: "Such was [1] the discernment of Mrs. Wilkins, and such [2] the respect she bore her master, [3] under whom she enjoyed a most excellent place, that her scruples gave way to his peremptory commands." Or we are told why Tom avoids a fight with Blifil: "for besides that [1] Tommy Jones was an inoffensive lad amidst all his roguery; and [2] really loved Blifil, [3] Mr. Thwackum being always the second of the latter, would have been sufficient to deter him." Substantiating the apparent multiplicity of motives is the author's pose of ignorance: "I know not for what reason" Jenny jumps up when Mrs. Partridge enters the room where she and Partridge are studying Latin. Wherever we turn we encounter the word "perhaps" or phrases such as "a matter not so easy to be accounted for," "we will not determine," or "I shall leave the reader to determine." All this is the counterpart of the doubt, confusion, and lack of subordination that characterizes the nonironic Richardsonian realism.

It is easy enough to take "Black George really loved Tom" as an ambiguity, but in the cases where Fielding lists multiple possibilities and says, "Take them all," one detects the pose of the Socratic ironist. In the examples concerning Mrs. Wilkins and Tom above, (1) and (2) are commendable motives, but (3) is prudential and has the effect of exposing the other two as rationalizations. All of the author's alternatives simply point to the ironic recognition that Mrs. Wilkins obeys out of fear for her position and that Tom is shy of the birch. Again, the author's ignorance is surely a mock-ignorance when he mediates on the motive of Allworthy's friend in recommending Thwackum as a tutor: "doubtless" because of Thwackum's qualifications of learning and religion, "though indeed" the friend was M.P. for a borough controlled by Thwackum's family.

The author is revealing a discrepancy between words (or rationalizations) and deeds that is not unlike the exposure of Square behind Molly Seagrim's arras. He asks the reader to pass judgment on Mrs. Wilkins, Tom, and the friend of Allworthy. But the very recording of multiple motives and qualifying clauses invites the reader to embrace them in his assessment; and acceptance of the invitation is made easy in many instances by the fact that the truth, or a missing portion of truth, is not revealed until hundreds of pages later. The basic unit in *Joseph Andrews* is the word contradicted by action or by the revelation of motive, and this same contradiction takes place in *Tom Jones,* eventually. But the latter, unlike *Joseph Andrews,* deals in suspense and surprise, with facts and actions long unknown to the reader; thus the emphasis falls not on the contradiction but on the speaker's speculations of the moment—which, though solidified later, nevertheless give to the novel an air of complexity and doubt which is not swept away by the denouement. When we see Bridget Allworthy showing generosity and kindness to little Tommy

Jones (deviating from the pattern of the Wilkins-like harpy we believe her to be), we feel that here is a real person, not a type. And when we eventually discover the "truth" this impression is not wiped out. Her prudence, like Wilkins's, is made to appear no longer a ruling passion but only one aspect of a multifaceted personality.

Irony is transformed by Fielding from a satiric strategy to a technique for suggesting the complexity of reality and the mitigating forces that make the "mixed" character in whom he is most interested, without succumbing to what he considered the chaos that accompanied Richardson's method, without abrogating judgment. Fielding's constant aim is to keep the reader from actually participating in the action, but have him merge himself in the author as a judge who can sympathize with the characters but never lose perspective on their actions. The psychological purpose of his irony is always subordinate to the analytic.

Tom Jones: The Argument of Design

Martin C. Battestin

FORTUNE AND PROVIDENCE

Design . . . implies an artificer. The assertion of Order and Harmony in the Creation entails the correlative belief in God's superintending Providence: as Pope has it, Nature is Art; Chance, Direction. Whereas the *Essay on Man* declares this doctrine discursively, a fundamental purpose of *Tom Jones* is to *demonstrate* it in the dramatic and representational mode of a comic fiction, which is—at least as Fielding practised the form—the symbolic imitation and epitome of life. Just as the methods of historical criticism have helped to clarify the meaning of design in *Tom Jones,* enabling us to grasp the full implication of Aristotle for the Augustan artist, so they may help us to come to terms with the vexed question of "probability" in Fielding's plot—as, indeed, in such other eighteenth-century fictions as *The Vicar of Wakefield* and *Roderick Random.*

Fielding declares in *Tom Jones* that the true province of the novelist is the "probable," not the "marvellous," even averring that he would rather see his hero hang than rescue him by unnatural means. But few critics have taken him seriously. In response to Coleridge's famous dictum that, together with *Oedipus Tyrannus* and *The Alchemist, Tom Jones* has one of the most perfect plots in literature, Austin Dobson long ago protested that:

From *The Augustan Milieu: Essays Presented to Louis A. Landa,* edited by Henry Knight Miller, Eric Rothstein, and G. S. Rousseau. © 1970 by Oxford University Press.

> Progress and animation alone will not make a perfect plot, unless probability be superadded. And though it cannot be said that Fielding disregards probability, he certainly strains it considerably. Money is conveniently lost and found; the naïvest coincidences continually occur; people turn up in the nick of time at the exact spot required and develop the most needful (but entirely casual) relations with the characters.

Although Professor Crane has gone far toward demonstrating that the action of *Tom Jones* may be seen as an "intricate scheme of probabilities," yet his inclusion of so many "accidents of Fortune" within this scheme does indeed strain, as Dobson put it, the definition of what is "probable." Certainly Fielding's practice in the novel seems often to belie his professions. What, we may well wonder, is perfect and probable about a plot which depends for its complication and happy resolution upon such a remarkable series of chance encounters and fortunate discoveries? Fleeing from her father's house, Sophia happens upon the one person who can direct her along the road that Tom has taken. Tom happens to find himself in that isolated region where both the Man of the Hill and Mrs. Waters are threatened by ruffians, and so is able to rescue them. Having been seduced by this rustic Circe, he later discovers that she is (as he has been told) his mother! Disconsolate when he learns that Sophia knows of his infidelity and has spurned him, he resolves to lose his life in defence of Hanover, but his plans are changed when he chances to fall into the same road his mistress has taken and chances to meet a beggar who has found the pocketbook she inadvertently dropped. Later, languishing in prison, he finds that he has not, after all, committed incest and that Mr. Fitzpatrick has not, after all, died of his wounds. Indeed, the incidence of such happy casualties in Fielding's plot has led critics deeper and more recent than Dobson to pronounce "Fortune" the sovereign deity of *Tom Jones*, "Fantasy" the wishful refuge of its author. Fielding *knew* the hard realities and tragic consequences of life, wherein handsome young men, however good-natured, are ruined by knaves and hanged for their indiscretions; but his sanguine humour was forever compelling him to turn the nightmare of actuality into a cheerful dream of Eden: something like this is the drift of too many modern readers.

What I wish here to suggest is that the fortunate contingencies and surprising turns which affect the course of events in *Tom Jones* are neither the awkward shifts of incompetency nor the pleasant fantasies of romance; rather, they have an essential function in the expression of Fielding's

Christian vision of life. As the general frame and architecture of *Tom Jones* is the emblem of Design in the macrocosm, so the narrative itself is the demonstration of Providence, the cause and agent of that Design. Unlike Defoe or Richardson, Fielding rejected the methods of "formal realism" for a mode which verges on the symbolic and allegorical: his characters and actions, though they have a life and integrity of their own, frequently demand to be read as tokens of a reality larger than themselves; his novels may be seen as artful and highly schematic paradigms of the human condition. For Fielding, and for the great majority of his contemporaries, no assumption about the world, and about man's place in the world, was more fundamental than the doctrine of a personal and particular Providence: "the belief of this," Tillotson had insisted, "is the great foundation of religion." This is the theme of countless discourses and homilies, most of which base their arguments on the discernible Order in the natural world and on the precepts of scripture. If we are to understand the significance of certain crucial recurrent themes in *Tom Jones*—the question of *probability* in the action of the novel and of *fortune* as it affects the lives of the characters—it will be useful to consider the doctrine of Providence as it appears in such representative authors as William Sherlock, whose *Discourse Concerning the Divine Providence* (1694) was a standard treatise on the subject, and those influential divines, Barrow, South, Tillotson, and Clarke, whose works Fielding is known to have read and admired.

Deriving ultimately from Aristotle and Horace, the critical principle of "probability" was first systematically applied to the novel by Fielding himself in *Tom Jones,* and—with the notable exception of the literature of the absurd—it has remained a basic operative principle with critics and novelists alike. Unlike the writer of romance, the novelist must decline the favours of gods from machines; his plot must work itself out by means of the natural interaction of the characters, the plausible and inevitable sequence of cause and effect. Fielding presents the doctrine most clearly in the prefatory chapter to book 17, as he considers the difficulties of extricating his hero from "the Calamities in which he is at present involved, owing to his Imprudence":

> This I faithfully promise, that notwithstanding any Affection, which we may be supposed to have for this Rogue, whom we have unfortunately made our Heroe, we will lend him none of that supernatural Assistance with which we are entrusted, upon Condition that we use it only on very important Oc-

casions. If he doth not therefore find some natural Means of
fairly extricating himself from all his Distresses, we will do
no Violence to the Truth and Dignity of History for his Sake;
for we had rather relate that he was hanged at *Tyburn* (which
may very probably be the Case) than forfeit our Integrity, or
shock the Faith of our Reader.

Yet what is "natural" or "probable" about the extraordinary chain
of events by which Jones is redeemed from prison and reconciled to his
friend and mistress, "crimes" undone, his enemies exposed, his true
identity revealed? As we have seen, "faith" of more than one reader has
been "shocked" by the apparent contrivance of Fielding's story. In another sense, however, the reader's faith—both in the ingenuity and kindly
art of the author (his wonderful ability to make everything come right
in the end) and in a corresponding benignity and design in the world he
is imitating—is confirmed and substantiated by this very contrivance.
Though Fielding spurned the good offices of the deus ex machina, he
warmly affirmed the benevolent Providence of the god *in* the machine,
that "vast Machine" to which he had earlier compared the world. He
could do so, moreover, without violating the critical principle he had
himself laid down. In a universe ultimately "comic" and Christian, the
occurrence of what William Turner called "*the Most Remarkable Provi-
dences, both of Judgment and Mercy*" was both natural and probable. To
write a novel—at least a comic novel—and fail to imply them would be,
in effect, to misrepresent the creation, to belie "what really exists."

Consider, for example, Tillotson's analysis in his sermon, "Success
not always Answerable to the Probability of Second Causes": though
"prudence," that virtue which Tom Jones so notably lacked, is necessary
in human life, since "GOD generally permits things to take their natural
course, and to fall out according to the power and probability of second
causes," yet "GOD hath reserved to himself a power and liberty to interpose, and to cross as he pleases, the usual course of things; to awaken
men to the consideration of him, and a continual dependance upon him;
and to teach us to ascribe those things to his wise disposal, which, if we
never saw any change, we should be apt to impute to blind necessity."
When prudence fails—prudence, which is the judicious weighing of
means to accomplish a desired end according to the probability of second
causes—then we must "look above and beyond these to a superior cause
which over-rules, and steers, and stops, as he pleases, all the motions and
activity of second causes. . . . For the providence of GOD doth many

times step in to divert the most probable event of things, and to turn it quite another way: and whenever he pleaseth to do so, the most strong and likely means do fall lame, or stumble, or by some accident or other come short of their end." This, too, is the burden of Samuel Clarke's sermon, "The Event of Things not always answerable to Second Causes": "the *Providence of God,* by means of *natural Causes,* which are all entirely of *His* appointment, and *Instruments only* in *His* hand; does often for wise reasons in his government of the World, disappoint the most probable expectations." With characteristic shrewdness, Robert South, whose wit Fielding could on occasion prefer to that of Congreve, managed his own extreme formulation of this doctrine. In his sermon, "On the Mercy of God," he presents a sort of Sartrean universe, wherein the accidental and adventitious are the rule rather than the exception: paradoxically, the improbable is the probable. Only the benevolent supervention of God prevents human life from being a monstrous succession of unpredictable calamities:

> How many are the casual unforeseen dangers, that the hand
> of Providence rescues [men] from! How many little things
> carry in them the causes of death! and how often are men that
> have escaped, amazed that they were not destroyed! Which
> shows that there is an eye that still watches over them, that
> always sees, though it is not seen; that knows their strengths
> and their weaknesses; where they are safe, and where they may
> be struck; and in how many respects they lie open to the
> invasion of a sad accident. . . . In a word, every man lives by
> a perpetual deliverance; a deliverance, which for the unlikeli-
> hood of it he could not expect, and for his own unworthiness,
> I am sure, he could not deserve.

In another well-known sermon, "All Contingencies under the Direction of God's Providence," South further insists that what men call Fortune and Chance are in fact nothing more than agents of God's wise government of the world, affecting everything that happens to us down even to the casting of lots.

The idea of Fortune is, indeed, a controlling theme in *Tom Jones.* It affects every stage in the hero's life from his birth to his imprisonment to his final redemption and marriage. To Allworthy, Tom is "a Child sent by Fortune to my Care." Before accepting his own responsibility for the calamities which have befallen him, Tom exclaims against the fickle goddess who has tormented him: "Sure . . . Fortune will never have done with me, 'till she hath driven me to Distraction." As we have remarked, the direction of Fielding's plot is frequently determined by the most unlikely coincidences, to which the narrator calls our attention in wry tribute to the goddess who "seldom doth Things by Halves." As we follow what Professor Crane has called the "intricate scheme of probabilities" leading through complication to final resolution, we are never allowed to forget another, equally significant aspect of the plot: that it is Fielding who is contriving the circumstances and manipulating the characters, violating the rules of probability in a deliberate and self-conscious manner, introducing into his own story an element of the improbable analogous to those unexpected and inexplicable occurrences in the actual world which come under the category of "luck." It is "Fortune," who, "having diverted herself, according to Custom, with two or three Frolicks, at last disposed all Matters to the Advantage of" Sophia as she plans to flee her father's house. It is "luck" which brings her to the same town and inn from which Jones had started on his journey, and which causes her to stumble on the same guide who had conducted him toward Bristol. It is the "lucky Circumstance" of Western's arrival in the nick of time that prevents Lord Fellamar's rape of Sophia. It is "Fortune," who, "after so many Disappointments," brings Tom and Sophia together again in Lady Bellaston's house, and "Fortune" again who appears "an utter Enemy" to their marriage. As he introduces his hero's ill-timed visit to Mr. Nightingale, the narrator summarizes this theme in the novel:

> Notwithstanding the Sentiment of the *Roman* Satirist, which denies the Divinity of *Fortune,* and the Opinion of *Seneca* to the same Purpose; *Cicero,* who was, I believe, a wiser Man than either of them, expressly holds the contrary; and certain it is, there are some Incidents in Life so very strange and unaccountable, that it seems to require more than human Skill and Foresight in producing them.

As Tillotson, as well as Cicero, was aware, there are limits to the efficacy of human prudence, an unpredictable and *apparently* irrational shape to circumstances.

Nowhere in the novel is this point more clearly and deliberately made than in the sequence of events which befall Fielding's hero immediately after Upton. Aware that his indiscretion with Mrs. Waters is known to Sophia, who has consequently abandoned him in dismay and indignation, Jones sets out from the inn convinced that his love is hopeless and resolved to give his life in the war against the Jacobites. Fortune, however, intervenes to change his purpose and lead him in pursuit of his mistress. The operation of Chance in human affairs is first demonstrated, appropriately enough, at a crossroads. Western, arriving at this junction in his efforts to overtake his daughter, "at last gave the Direction of his Pursuit to Fortune, and struck directly into the *Worcester* Road," which leads him away from Sophia; confronted with the same choice, Jones, still determined to join the King's forces, "immediately struck into the different Road from that which the Squire had taken, and, by mere Chance, pursued the very same thro' which *Sophia* had before passed." Reaching another cross-way, Jones and Partridge there encounter an illiterate beggar who, in travelling the same road Sophia had taken, happened to find the little pocketbook containing a £100 bank-note which she had accidentally dropped. This chance discovery provides Jones both with a motive to pursue Sophia and with the guide he needs to resolve the difficulty of the crossroads. Of this fortunate coincidence—and a later one equally lucky—Partridge points the obvious moral: "'two such Accidents could never have happened to direct him after his Mistress, if Providence had not designed to bring them together at last.' And this [the narrator observes] was the first Time that *Jones* lent any Attention to the superstitious Doctrines of his Companion."

The episode of the beggar at the crossroads serves as a sort of parable of the doctrine of Providence which Fielding affirms throughout *Tom Jones.* Finding himself by chance in that remote place where the Man of the Hill is threatened by thieves, Jones comes to the rescue and acknowledges himself to be the instrument of God: "'Be thankful then,' cries *Jones,* 'to that Providence to which you owe your Deliverance.'" As he takes his leave of the Old Man, Jones's "providential Appearance" at the scene of Northerton's attempted murder of Mrs. Waters enables him to perform a similar office, no less pious than gallant, by rescuing the damsel from distress, and confessing himself "highly pleased with the extraordinary Accident which had sent him thither for her Relief, where it was so improbable she should find any; adding, that Heaven seemed to have designed him as the happy Instrument of her Protection." Such "extraordinary accidents" and happy improbabilities are not so much a convenience to Fielding the author, providing him with easy escapes from the difficulties of his plot, as they are a calculated demonstration of providential care and design in the world. Most of these coincidences in *Tom Jones* are so gratuitous that an author of Fielding's inventive skill could easily have avoided them: Jones's rescue of the Old Man, for example, serves no real function either in advancing the plot or in allowing the two characters to meet, since Jones and Partridge have already settled themselves in the Old Man's house before the attack occurs; and there were a score of devices more probable than the chance encounter with a lucky beggar at a crossroads which Fielding might have used to put his hero on the trail of Sophia. Jones in the first case and the beggar in the second are agents not only of their author in administering the narrative, but also of that higher Providence for which, within the symbolic microcosm of the novel, the author stands as surrogate. Fielding's contrivances imply those of the Deity.

The theme of Providence is—somewhat paradoxically it may seem to us—enforced by those recurrent, intrusive references to Fortune that we have earlier remarked. For the modern reader the two concepts appear contradictory; for Fielding and his contemporaries, however, they were two ways of conveying the same idea, of acknowledging that "more than human Skill and Foresight" which alone could produce the "strange and unaccountable" casualties of life. Fortune (or Chance) was, indeed, no more than a figure of speech, a convenient vulgarism, enabling one to talk of Providence while avoiding the note of pious sobriety—a note well lost in the pages of a comic novel. "As to *Chance*," declared Samuel Clarke, "'tis evident That is nothing but a *mere Word*, or an *abstract Notion* in our manner of conceiving things. It has no real Being; it is Nothing, and can *do* nothing." Or again, in his sermon "The Event of Things not always answerable to Second Causes," Clarke denounces the Epicurean notion that Chance, not Design, governs the world: "We may observe, that what men vulgarly call *Chance* or unforeseen *Accident*, is in Scripture always declared to be the *determinate Counsel and Providence of God.* What careless and inconsiderate men ascribe in common Speech to *Chance* or *Fortune;* that is, to *nothing at all*, but a mere empty word, signifying only their *Ignorance* of the true Causes of things; this the Scripture teaches *Us* to ascribe to the all-seeing and all-directing Providence of God." Perhaps the most illuminating gloss on the theme of Fortune and Providence in *Tom Jones*, however, is found in William Sherlock's *Discourse Concerning the Divine Providence*, a work popular enough to have gone through nine editions by 1747. Sherlock's third chapter, "*Concerning God's* Governing Providence," anticipates Fielding's parable of the lost-and-found banknote, using the same example to illustrate the dominion of Fortune over the affairs of men and the dominion of Providence over Fortune:

> Let us consider God's Government of accidental Causes, or what we call Chance and Accident, which has a large Empire

over human Affairs: Not that Chance and Accident can do any Thing, properly speaking; for whatever is done, has some proper and natural Cause which does it; but what we call Accidental Causes, is rather such an Accidental Concurrence of different Causes, as produces unexpected and undesigned Effects; as when one Man by Accident loses a Purse of Gold, and another Man walking in the Fields without any such Expectation, by as great an Accident finds it. And how much of the Good and Evil that happens to us in this World, is owing to such undesigned, surprizing, accidental Events, every Man must know, who has made any Observations on his own, or other Mens Lives and Fortunes. . . . *Time and Chance,* some favourable Junctures, and unseen Accidents, are more powerful than all human Strength, or Art, or Skill.

Now what an ill State were Mankind in, did not a wise and merciful Hand govern what we call Chance and Fortune? How can God govern the World, or dispose Mens Lives and Fortunes without governing Chance, all unseen, unknown, and surprizing Events, which disappoint the Counsels of the Wise, and in a Moment unavoidably change the whole Scene of Human Affairs? Upon what little unexpected Things do the Fortunes of Men, of Families, of whole Kingdoms turn? And unless these little unexpected Things are governed by God, some of the greatest Changes in the World are exempted from his Care and Providence.

This is Reason enough to believe, That if God governs the World, he governs Chance and Fortune; that the most unexpected Events, how casual soever they appear to us, are foreseen and ordered by God.

Such events as these are the properest Objects of God's Care and Government; because they are very great Instruments of Providence; many times the greatest Things are done by them, and they are the most visible Demonstration of a superior Wisdom and Power which governs the World.

As Sherlock postulates and Fielding in *Tom Jones* dramatizes, a lost purse, a dropped pocketbook—however adventitious they may appear—find a place in God's benevolent ordering of things.

Sherlock also anticipates Fielding in defining the relationship between Fortune and human foresight, Providence and Prudence—the one

sustaining the frame of the world and guiding the affairs of men according to the dictates of perfect Wisdom, the other imitating the example of
this divine wisdom, however fallibly, in the sphere of the individual life.
As the passage opens, we may recall Fielding's allusion to Cicero:

> The Heathens made Fortune a Goddess, and attributed the
> Government of all Things to her. . . . Whereby they only sig-
> nified the Government of Providence in all casual and fortui-
> tous Events; and if Providence governs any Thing, it must
> govern Chance, which governs almost all Things else, and
> which none but God can govern. As far as Human Prudence
> and Foresight reaches, God expects we should take care of
> ourselves; and if we will not, he suffers us to reap the Fruits
> of our own Folly; but when we cannot take care of ourselves,
> we have reason to expect and hope, that God will take care
> of us. In other Cases, human Prudence and Industry must
> concur with the Divine Providence: In Matters of Chance and
> Accident, Providence must act alone, and do all itself, for we
> know nothing of it; so that all the Arguments for Providence,
> do most strongly conclude for God's Government of all casual
> Events.

Though God allows scope for the voluntary acts of men—who, in so far
as they conduct themselves virtuously, with charity and prudence, have
fulfilled their duty to their neighbours and themselves—He none the less
controls the whole Creation with unerring wisdom and omniscience,
ordering even the bungling and malicious deeds of human beings within
the fabric of His wise design. As Clarke expressed it, "'tis impossible
but he must actually direct and appoint every particular thing and circumstance that is in the World or ever shall be, excepting only what by
his own pleasure he puts under the Power and Choice of subordinate
Free Agents." "Nor is there *in Nature* Any *Other Efficient* or proper *Cause*
of any Event . . . but only the *Free Will of rational and intelligent* Creatures,
acting within the Sphere of their limited Faculties; and the *Supreme Power
of God,* directing, by his omnipresent Providence . . . the inanimate Motions of the whole material and unintelligent World." Within *Tom Jones*
both these assumptions about reality are accommodated: on the one
hand, we may trace, with Professor Crane, what might be termed the
"naturalistic" determination of events through the probable and predict-
able interaction of the characters; yet, on the other hand, we are aware
of what seems best described as the "artificial" determination of events

through the arbitrary and quite improbable contrivances of the author, who presides like Providence over the world of the novel, distant yet very much involved, omniscient and all-powerful, arranging the elements and circumstances of his story according to a preconceived scheme as symmetrical and benevolent as the Design of that larger Creation he mirrors.

The shape of Fielding's narrative in *Tom Jones* and his choice of a narrative method may thus be seen as, in a sense, inevitable: the perfect vehicles for his theme. This theme, the assertion of Design and Providence in the world, is indeed the basis of Fielding's comic vision. It echoes in his writings from *The Champion* to that refutation of Bolingbroke which he died too soon to finish. God was always for him "the only true, great Ruler of the Universe, who is a Being of infinite Justice," a Being "supremely wise and good," who was concerned to reward the virtuous and punish the guilty, and "in whose Power is the Disposition of all Things." He could scoff at those atheists and freethinkers who, like Epicurus or Mandeville, preferred to believe against the dictates of reason "that this vast regular Frame of the Universe, and all the artful and cunning Machines therein were the Effects of Chance, of an irregular Dance of Atoms." Such perfection in the works of Nature, he declared in another leader, was "infinitely superior to all the little Quackery, and impotent Imitation of Art." But always for Fielding this nice Design in the Creation implied the continuing care of the Artificer, whose hand controlled the fates of nations and of individual men: in *The Jacobite's Journal* (March 19, 1748) he printed with approval a letter from a correspondent who observed that it was God's "good and all-directing Providence" which had freed England from Stuart tyranny and established her Constitution; and a similar conviction informs his little chronicle of divine retribution, *Examples of the Interposition of Providence in the Detection and Punishment of Murder* (1752). What Fielding himself affirms is, moreover, reiterated by the good men and women of his fiction, who express their trust in Providence in their adversity or their gratitude to God for their timely deliverances. Appropriately enough, it is Parson Adams who best summarizes this doctrine when, echoing Tillotson and a score of other divines, he admonishes Joseph Andrews in affliction: with Joseph we are reminded that "no Accident happens to us without the Divine Permission," that "the same Power which made us, rules over us, and we are absolutely at his Disposal"; but, while acknowledging God's omnipotence, we may take comfort in the knowledge that every accident, every event, is "ultimately directed" to some benevolent purpose. In Fielding's last novel it is Amelia who echoes the parson's faith, acknowledging "that Divine Will and Pleasure, without whose Permission at least, no Human Accident can happen."

As in the world at large, the "ultimate direction" of events in *Tom Jones*—and, indeed, in all Fielding's novels—is a comic apocalypse: that last, improbable, joyous catastrophe in which true identities are discovered, the innocent redeemed, an unerring justice meted out to one and all. To use South's fine phrase, the "perpetual deliverance" of Fielding's characters from rape, murder, imprisonment, disgrace, is the essential pattern of his fiction—a pattern culminating in the final distribution of poetic justice. Yet one of the absurdities which Fielding found in *Pamela* was Richardson's insistence that virtue was rewarded and vice punished in this world: "A very wholesome and comfortable Doctrine," Fielding remarked in *Tom Jones,* "and to which we have but one Objection, namely, That it is not true." Why, one may well ask, should the happy conclusion of Fielding's own fiction be considered any less intellectually reprehensible than that of *Pamela*? The answer, I believe, is implicit in what we have been saying so far about the relation of form to meaning in *Tom Jones.* Whereas Richardson offers *Pamela* to us as a literal transcription of reality, Fielding's intention is ultimately symbolic. In the preface to *Joseph Andrews* Fielding saw the business of the comic novelist, as he saw that of his friend Hogarth, the "Comic History-Painter," 'as "the exactest copying of Nature"; but he meant this in an Aristotelian, not a Baconian, sense. He would have agreed with Imlac that the poet was not concerned to number the streaks of the tulip; his subject was "not Men, but Manners; not an Individual, but a Species." Richardson's eye is on the fact, Fielding's on the abstraction which the fact implies. The happy ending of *Pamela* is unacceptable because the novel asks to be taken as a faithful (even in a pious sense) representation of actuality. Fielding's fiction makes no such claim. Ultimately he asks us to consider not Tom Jones, but "HUMAN NATURE," not so much the story of his hero's fall and redemption as that rational and benign scheme of things which the story and its witty, genial author imply. *Tom Jones* asks to be taken as a work of Art, as paradigm and emblem of that wise Design which Pope celebrated, and in terms of which, "partial Evil," however real, however terrible, may be seen as "universal Good." Given this assumption of an order and meaning to life, there must be, as Samuel Clarke put it, a

> final vindication of the Honour and Laws of God in the proportionable reward of the best, or punishment of the worst of Men. And consequently 'tis certain and necessary . . . there

must at some time or other be such a Revolution and Reno-
vation of Things, such a *future State* of existence of the same
Persons, as that by an exact distribution of Rewards or Punishments therein, all the present Disorders and Inequalities
may be set right; and that the whole Scheme of Providence,
which to us who judge of it by only one small Portion of it,
seems now so inexplicable and much confused; may appear at
its consummation, to be a Design worthy of Infinite Wisdom,
Justice and Goodness.

Within the microcosm of the novel, this is precisely the function of Fielding's comic denouements, at which, miraculously, every difficulty is
swept away, every inequity redressed. What appeared confusion, both in
the conduct of the story and in the lives of the characters, is, after all, a
wise design: the mighty maze is not without a plan. And a principal
instrument of this revelation is an astonishing sequence of what Fielding
calls "those strange Chances, whence very good and grave Men have
concluded that Providence often interposes in the Discovery of the most
secret Villainy." Sharing Allworthy's admiration at the "wonderful
Means" by which mysteries have been dispelled and justice has
triumphed, the reader may wish to apply to Fielding himself what the
good squire exclaims of the Deity: "Good Heavens! Well! the Lord dis-
poseth all Things."

In the deliberate, philosophic use of coincidence, if in no other respect, Fielding reminds us of no one so much as Thomas Hardy—
though, to be sure, the intentions of the two novelists are antithetical.
Whereas the grotesque improbabilities of Hardy's plots are meant to mirror a universe hostile, or at best indifferent, to man, Fielding's happy
turns and fortunate encounters reflect a very different, appropriately Augustan world. His contrivances, as we have remarked, imply those of the
Deity. Fielding was not, of course, alone among his contemporaries in
enforcing this analogy. As Richard Tyre has shown, it was a fundamental
argument with such critics as John Dennis for whom poetic justice in the
drama was necessary as the reflection of "meaning, order, and coherence"
in the universe. Neither Dennis nor Fielding was blind to the tragic
circumstances of life, but both conceived the function of art to be the
imitation of a reality more comprehensive and rational than our limited
experience could disclose: "Poetick Justice," Dennis observed, "would
be a Jest if it were not an Image of the Divine, and if it did not consequently suppose the Being of a God and Providence." A similar rationale,

I believe, underlies that extraordinary series of calamities and fortunate restorations which modern critics have deplored in the plot of Goldsmith's Christian fable, *The Vicar of Wakefield*; and Smollett, too—though in a much more arbitrary and perfunctory fashion—attempts to justify the preposterous turns and discoveries of *Roderick Random* by attributing them all to the marvellous workings of Providence. Written from a comparable belief in a Christian universe, such works as *Troilus and Criseyde, Paradise Lost,* and *Clarissa* attempt to reconcile the tragedy of existence with the consoling doctrine of the Church by resorting, variously, to a final apotheosis of the hero or to the reassurances of a ministering angel.

Happily, no such solution is possible or necessary to the comic novelist. As the example of Smollett in *Roderick Random,* or of Osborne in the film of *Tom Jones,* makes clear, nothing, of course, is less artistically satisfying than a happy ending incoherently imposed on a story, whereby chance medley at a stroke becomes a wedding feast. The marriage of Tom and Sophia, however, is the *telos* of Fielding's novel, standing in the same relation to the world of *Tom Jones* as that "Great Day" toward which life itself was tending, "when," as Clarke expressed it, "the Reasons of things and the whole Counsel of God shall be more perfectly disclosed." *Tom Jones* has been cherished for many reasons, but its special triumph is as a work of art: the form of the novel—its symmetry of design; the artful contrivance of its plot; the intrusive, omniscient narrator; and that final, miraculous resolution of every complication—is the expression and emblem of its author's coherent, Christian vision of life.

Glory, Jest, and Riddle:
The Masque of Tom Jones in London

Grete Ek

The narrator of *Tom Jones,* it is well known, conceives of his story as a vast theatrical performance, constructed on the analogy with life itself, and as master of the show he assigns parts, directs action, and moves his puppets between locations. The text thus provides a major example of what we may call a translation of the theatrical metaphor into narrative technique of a kind current both in the visual arts and the fiction of the eighteenth century. The theatrical mode, Ronald Paulson has recently argued, merges with an adaptation of the journey motif, and in Hogarth as in Fielding or Goldsmith the hero's progress is presented as a journey from one act to the next. It is also a pattern which recalls, and with particular insistence, the second half of *Don Quixote,* where most significant incidents take the form of actual performances or plays-within, be it a troupe of actors impersonating the Parliament of Death, the Bachelor Sampson Carrasco posing as a Herculean Knight of the Mirrors, a theatrical wedding ceremony, or a puppet show staged by Maese Pedro. *Praxis,* in other words, becomes with considerable consistency a string of one-act plays, at least one step removed from the surrounding narrative. It is clear that the device of the interpolated performance has migrated into Fielding's text and has turned into another puppet show, a masquerade, a staging of *Hamlet*. Equally important and striking is the string of nondigressive or causally related incidents presented as roles to be played or guises and shapes and masks to be put on by those puppets which we label "characters." It is problems relating to the presentation

From *English Studies* 60, no. 2 (April 1979). © 1979 by Swets & Zeitlinger, B. V.

of character within a narrative structure of this order that my paper will attempt to discuss—not of course as a general issue, which would carry much too far within the present context, but as a subject arising from one specific textual problem.

Although no serious critic would claim that character psychology is a primary consideration in a Fielding text, most of us assume that the various parts played by minor and major puppets are supposed to add up according to some principle of coherence and become integral elements in an entity labelled Tom, or Sophia, or Blifil. By contrast, Jonathan Wild does not add up at all: as I see it, he appears in two major but mutually contradictory roles that each spans roughly one half of the text. The details of what are in effect two separate narratives parallel one another with striking exactness and lead to complementary ends (shipwreck and hanging), the different degree of seriousness in type of incident reflecting the very different types of motivation within the two sequences (self-love and pure malice). But then such change of masks is germane to satire as a genre, and it would be absurd to blame Jonathan for being next-of-kin to Captain Gulliver. Tom Jones is another matter altogether, apparently also to "Fielding," who speaks of the necessity for "conservation" of character. The performance—or rather different performances—of Tom within the first half of the London sequence takes us to the heart of the problem. Two interlocking narrative strands, which terminate at approximately the same point present the hero in what appear to be morally incompatible roles, as reprobate and champion of virtue respectively. It is of course a duality prefigured by the basic structure of his character, but its manifestations are too extreme to be explained by implications in the original portrait and by previous actions. The liaison with Lady Bellaston, who pays generously for Tom's services, is quite simply not very nice, and far less acceptable than grotto excursions with Molly Seagrim or temporary bliss in the arms of the voluptuous Mrs Waters in the inn at Upton. Within the novel's ethical construct, it becomes the ultimate fall. At the same time, Tom's labours on behalf of the Millers make him a truly efficacious moral agent, and bestow upon him the distinction of Virtue incarnate. It is a kind of moral ascent, and a logical sequel to that trial scene which terminates the hero's wanderings on the road, and in which he metaphorically ascends the bench and assumes the magisterial role of Allworthy himself. Tom, then, alternates between the extremes of descent and ascent—a point which has not to my knowledge come in for attention. So far, two major approaches to the notorious Bellaston episode seem to have crystallized.

One is to deplore it as artistically unfortunate, another to emphasize artifice in a positive sense and to consider it a "momentary and rectifiable indiscretion." My argument will claim that Tom's pattern of behaviour within the relevant textual segments may be seen as part of a system of heroic theatricals. It will suggest (not define, which is an obvious impossibility) a referential dimension to the performances given by Tom, based on the thesis that they are heroic, specifically "Herculean" poses with an internal structure deriving from an archetype. The major premise of such an argument is the belief that a particular textual element—in this case a type of action or sequence of such actions—may receive much of its thematic import and functional significance from the ceaseless dialogue it conducts with its models. Finally, there will be an attempt to approach the subject character/mask as a crossroads of technical and thematic interests.

The relationship between Lady Bellaston and Tom could be summarily described as one between mistress and slave. We may suspect, therefore, that an underlying pattern is to be found in the enslavement of the heroic type, Hercules, to Omphale, Queen of Lydia. If less immediately popular than the Choice of Hercules—recently discussed as a potential model for the pattern of action in the central books of *Tom Jones*—the topos enjoyed rare currency and longevity and is classified as a comic archetype by Northrop Frye, who describes it as portraying "man bullied or dominated by women." Presumably *Jonathan Wild* draws on the same general model in the mock-heroic portrayal of the Great Man: he keeps turning up on Miss Laetitia Snap's doorstep, "for he had that weakness of suffering himself to be enslaved by women, so naturally incident to men of heroic disposition." The basic features of the classical story need to be briefly recapitulated. The earliest versions tersely recount how Hercules consented to be sold as a slave to the Queen of Lydia, whom he served for some period of time, while continuing to perform labours, like ridding the land of robbers. Later writers, notably Seneca, came to spell out the details of an adulterous relationship. In *Hercules Oetaeus,* the nurse of Deianeira, Hercules' lawful wife, speaks of the hero as "a wanderer in love":

> When a guest on Timolus, he caressed the Lydian woman and, daft with love, sat beside her swift distaff, twisting the moistened thread with doughty fingers. His shoulder, indeed, had laid aside the famous lion's-skin, a turban confined his hair, and there he stood like any slave, his shaggy locks dripping

with Sabean myrrh. Everywhere has he burned with love, but
burned with feeble flame.

A comic version of the story appears in Ovid's *Fasti,* where Faunus witnesses a beautiful Omphale attended by her enthralled slave Hercules—
and Omphale typically makes Hercules put on her own clothes. Finally,
the brief portraits presented by Fielding's favourite Lucian call for passing
attention. In the *Dialogues of the Gods* Asclepius taunts Hercules for his
onetime subjection to Omphale: "Besides, if nothing else, I was never a
slave like you, carding wool in Lydia, and being beaten with Omphale's
golden sandal." *How to Write History* includes a description of a painting
of Hercules and Omphale as a "shocking spectacle" in which Hercules'
"divine masculinity is disgracefully feminised."

In post-classical times, an astonishing number of works of art were
based directly on the story of Hercules and Omphale, most of which are
listed in Will Tissot's *Simson und Hercules in den Gestaltungen des Barock.*
This useful compilation indicates that the greater number of works—be
they operas, plays, or paintings—saw the light of day in the eighteenth
century. An exquisite Rubens picture, incidentally acquired by Sir Joshua
Reynolds during his second visit to Flanders in 1785, may serve as a good
example of Ovidian comic treatment pursued by modern artists: the spinning Hercules presents a very foolish appearance, and Omphale is busy
pinching his ear. Examining Tissot's catalogue, one notes that particularly in France at the beginning of the eighteenth century, the subject was
frequently given a purely comic form.

If Fielding's text does exploit what had become a paradigmatic incident, it would probably be directly indebted to classical sources, although part of the effect would be achieved through its interaction with
thematic dimensions established by modern usage. We know that Spenser
based part of *his* Legend of Justice, the Artegall-Radigund episode, on
the Hercules-Omphale story, but in a manner that echoes Renaissance
interpretations. A relatively recent argument sees Radigund as another
embodiment of the traditional Pleasure-figure that Hercules Prodicus
encountered at the crossways, and posits that Spenser ran together two
aspects of the Hercules myth, in the manner of for example Annibale
Carracci, whose companion pictures of the topoi "as it were put a sig-
nature to the similarity between Omphale and *voluptas.*" Renaissance
emblematists and mythographers made the equation with positive glee.
Thus Henry Peacham, illustrating the power of love, and describing the
spinning Hercules: he complains

> That all his conquests wonne him not such Fame,
> For which as God, the world did him adore,
> As Loues affection, did disgrace and shame
> His virtues partes. How many are there more,
> Who hauing Honor, and a worthy name,
> By actions base, and lewdness loose the same.

Alexander Ross casts himself in the role of pedagogue: the story is a warning to young men "that the end of pleasure is pain, and that love (or lust rather) which in the beginning is all honey, determines in gall and wormwood." The wages of sin is death indeed. A less insistent didacticism is expressed by a greater man, Natalis Comes. It is true that the tale was set down to posterity in order to restrain young men from submitting to Pleasure. But one deplorable incident cannot absolutely condemn an otherwise honourable character: "Et ne peut-on aussi qualifier aucun absoluëment homme de bien, s'il ne passe les iours de son estre iusques à la derniere heure auec une accomplie integrité de vie?" The eighteenth century does away with some of the more flamboyant rhetoric, but the concepts remain largely unaltered. In 1747 we find Joseph Spence commenting on the topos in familiar terms. Hercules was, unfortunately, a "slave to love," and the "chief scene of his effeminacies" was in the land of Omphale, where "he acted his low part the most notoriously" so that "All his dignity is (with much propriety) quite lost on this occasion." Banier's *Mythology*, generally an enemy to allegorization and extreme moralization of myths, presumably draws on Lucian and explains the notorious spinning as a metaphor for "a very effeminate and voluptous Life."

Unlike book 5 of *The Faerie Queene*, *Tom Jones* contains no overt references to an underlying model, but certain verbal clues are nonetheless suggestive of a referential framework. The epithet of "queen," liberally bestowed on Lady Bellaston in the masquerade scene and after, is an obvious case in point. Terms used to classify the relationship between Tom and his ageing paramour may be seen as allusive:

> [Tom] knew the tacit Consideration upon which all her Favours were conferred; and as his Necessity obliged him to accept them, so his Honour, he concluded, forced him to pay the Price. This therefore he resolved to do, whatever Misery it cost him, and to devote himself to her, from that great Principle of Justice, by which the Laws of some Countries

oblige a Debtor who is not otherwise capable of discharging
his Debt, to become the Slave of his Creditor.

Complementing the hero's moral awakening, the terminology changes
from potentially suggestive to unambiguously so: "Indeed he began to
look on all the Favours he had received, rather as Wages than Benefits,
which depreciated not only her, but himself too in his own Conceit."
Tom then decides to quit Lady Bellaston's "*Service, in which* Light he
now saw his Affair with her," and is finally "well satisfied with his
Deliverance from a Thraldom which those who have ever experienced it
will . . . allow to be none of the lightest." Words like "Service" and
"Thraldom" may serve as direct reminders of the heroic type, specifically
perhaps of the Herculean descendant Artegall. He endured a period
"Seruing proud *Radigund* with true subiection / How euer it his noble
heart did gall, / T'obay a womans tyrannous direction," and "Thus he
long while in thraldome there remayned," incurring the scorn of men
who "report of him much ill, / For yeelding so himselfe a wretched
thrall / To th'insolent commaund of womens will; / That all his former
praise doth fowly spill."

Secondly, a number of minor incidents may read as Fielding's adaptations of standard ingredients in the archetype. Tom, we remember, lays
off his own clothes. When entering London, he is dressed in a plain
fustian suit, and this sober habit is eventually replaced by more fashionable garments provided by the generosity of Lady Bellaston, so that "by
her Means he was now become one of the best dress'd Men about Town."
Tom has, in fact, temporarily joined the illustrious company of citified
fops who never failed to attract Fielding's ridicule. It is, I believe, not
fanciful to see the hero's change of clothes as a modern redaction of the
disgraceful feminization that Lucian spoke of—although Tom is not, of
course, literally dressed in "women's weeds." The distaff is mercifully
absent from eighteenth-century London. This aspect of the classical story
was, as we have seen, explicated by modern commentators like Banier
as a metaphor for a profoundly humiliating experience, whereby the hero
is made to assume a particularly ridiculous posture, and it was an incident
dear to comic writers and artists. Only in the London sequence does
Tom appear as a downright fool. Placed between Lady Bellaston and
Sophia, for example, the hero is "ready to sink with Fear. He sat kicking
his Heels, playing with his Fingers, and looking more like a Fool, if it
be possible, than a young booby Squire, when he is first introduced into
a polite Assembly." Two complementary bedroom scenes, with Lady

Bellaston and Honour alternately behind the curtain, turn the tables on Tom and reverse the situation of the memorable scene when the hero exposed the philosopher Square in Molly Seagrim's attic. This time it is Tom who plays the clown. His descent into Lady Bellaston's "moral sink" (Alter's term) becomes a ludicrous performance by which the hero is reduced to a fool, not unlike the comic Hercules subject to the whims of Omphale.

It is, however, primarily as a system of morally significant actions, or *praxis,* that the textual segments in question betray their kinship to the pattern of actions in the model I have been discussing. Tom literally sells himself to the "Queen of the Fairies," receiving money in return for services that clearly give him little pleasure, but which raise him "to a State of Affluence, beyond what he had ever known." It is an act which mimics that of the heroic type. Tom consents to his own enslavement, and his joyless peregrinations in my lady's bed become punishment rather than delectation. This interpretation may be based on the logic of the plot. Tom fails to meet Sophia at Upton because he is in bed with Mrs Waters, which again leads to his quest for her and to the meeting with Lady Bellaston; in other words, the affair with Mrs Waters leads to the affair with Lady Bellaston. If the former incident is foolish and the latter disagreeable, it follows that imprudence at Upton may be said to cause punishment in London. Enslavement in expiation of crimes committed is, as we have seen, a type of action found in the Herculean model. Further, Tom is bound to a wise and worthy woman, emotionally and morally, but consents to what becomes an adulterous relationship. The archetype, Hercules, was married to the faithful Deianeira, and his descendant, Artegall, is betrothed to Britomart, the female personification of wisdom (Sophy, as she is sometimes called). Once again Tom mimics the heroic model through the type of action he performs. By the same token, Lady Bellaston acts in a manner that may identify her as a type of Omphale; she refuses to give up her freedom to any man on earth (see her answer to Tom's proposal of marriage), and in a general way conforms to the image of the female despot that Omphale was thought to represent.

At a later stage, Tom is actually imprisoned, after events that with some exactness parallel the prelude to his Bellaston servitude. There is the quest for the Sophia he did not meet at Upton, another assignment with Mrs Fitzpatrick (we remember that she was the lady Tom expected to meet at the masquerade), another staged performance (*Hamlet* for masquerade), another confrontation as a result of false principles of honour (actual duel for sparring with Lady Bellaston). These are complementary sets of events that lead to two types of imprisonment, the second term of servitude being a physical realization of what was earlier a moral state. The central idea of bondage, then, receives further emphasis through its repetition in realistic terms.

Finally, and by far most importantly, the seemingly paradoxical nature of Tom's initial London progress, as translated into two parallel and partly interdependent narrative strands, reflects the basic structure of the classical story: the hero endures his period of servitude while performing labours in the interest of his fellow men. Both Fielding's text and the classical model combine moral descent and ascent, and a recognition of model will suggest that two seemingly contradictory roles are traditional aspects of heroic conduct, in this case of a deflated and comic variety. It would not be wrong to say that they are both parts of a moral paradigm, and take their place among other paradigmatic incidents in the modern epic, like for example the inevitable descent to the underworld (where the Irish peer's porter appears as "*Cerberus* the Porter of Hell") and the wielding of the rusty counterpart to the sword of virtue and justice. There is also a kind of logic involved which springs specifically from the moral geography of Fielding's text, and which comments ironically upon certain modern interpretations of the archetypal pattern woven into the narrative. For the Bellaston affair—Tom's ultimate fall—is turned into another labour, another test of heroic virtue, and as such congruent with his many labours on behalf of the unfortunate Millers. Rather than the type of sin that "determines in gall and wormwood" (we may be quite sure that Fielding would not have liked Alexander Ross, if he had read him!) Tom's basest act is integrated into a highly patterned process of learning, part of which is the acquisition of the ability to distinguish "things as they really are in themselves, not as they appear through the masks and disguises of fallacious semblance"—to use a passage from Isaac Barrow that Martin Battestin quotes in his admirable discussion of prudence in *Tom Jones*.

This is where it is important to see Lady Bellaston as a type of Pleasure/Vice, as Maren-Sofie Røstvig has suggested, an argument which tallies also with interpretations of the Hercules/Omphale story pointed to above. Lady Bellaston's physical unattractiveness ("once an Object of Desire," but now "entered at least into the Autumn of Life") is emblematic of her function as Pleasure/Vice appearing, finally, in her true colours as all foul. Tom is, then, fettered and enslaved to the most sinister embodiment of the "Pleasure" he served too willingly and joy-fully in the past, true Pleasure being, of course, reconciled with Virtue in the lovely Sophia. As he sees Lady Bellaston for what she is, and himself for what he becomes by serving her, he rejects her. And his third and final fall turns into the first of three rejections, which, almost ritu-alistically, undo his three transgressions. It should be noted in passing that his refusal of the wealthy widow Hunt is the outcome of a dilemma of a different order, one which posits a positive choice between two honourable ways of behaviour. It is presented as a full-scale psychomachia, and becomes his final choice of Sophia over any other woman. The plot reflects this: only after Sophia has been told of this particular incident is she willing to believe in Tom's love. The rejection of Lady Bellaston is part of another type of process, a negative one as it were, in the course of which different Vice-figures parade before Tom and are summarily dismissed. The first incident is set in book 15, chapter 9. In book 16, chapter 9, it is Mrs Fitzpatrick who assumes the role of Pleasure/Vice as Tom goes to visit her. The lady mimics Mrs Waters at Upton, particularly through her use of that language of the eyes in which Mrs Waters proved so adept during the seduction scene. This time, however, Tom has made his ultimate choice (the refusal of Mrs Hunt takes place in book 15, chapter 10), and "his whole Thoughts were now so confined to his *Sophia*, that . . . no Woman upon Earth could have drawn him into an Act of Inconstancy." He again rejects "Pleasure." The final rejection is set in book 17, chapter 9, when Mrs Waters herself turns up in Tom's cell, brimming with references to their union at Upton. She thus at first attempts to assume her old role. Tom, knowing Pleasure for what it is, rejects it for the third time. It will have been noted that these three typological acts are placed in the same chapter—the ninth—in three con-secutive books. No more should be needed to call attention to their interrelationship.

The Bellaston episode is, then, both literally and metaphorically a pivotal element in Fielding's text. It turns one particular aspect of the hero's moral progress all the way around through the fact that the inci-dent that represents the very deepest humiliation—the archetypal heroic fall—is also enlisted among the hero's labours, and becomes the first step in a serial process of moral repatriation. The ironic connotations implicit in the tension between the text of *Tom Jones* and possible models with their adaptations and interpretations can only be dimly perceived, for the referential framework is no invariant. I have called the relationship a "dialogue." As yet we have no methodological tools with which to approach it in a systematic way, but there is little sense in pretending that it does not exist.

The words "moral repatriation" have been chosen with some care. They indicate a somewhat "static" conception of character in Fielding, a view which is no longer pure heresy. This is a complex and large issue and cannot be pursued here. Suffice it to say that the basic structure of "Tom" is sketched at an early stage, and that the progress of the hero may be seen as a realization of potential through a learning process, without alternation in the essential composition of the portrait. This brings me to the final necessary consideration within the present context, namely the relationship—or lack of such—between the character of Tom in a more complete sense than considered so far and the heroic theatricals in which he is involved. We have seen that separate acts are interrelated and relevant to the hero's moral education, but the question whether there is correlation between the original portrait of Tom and the part he plays in the company of Lady Bellaston must still be answered in the negative. In his discussion of Fielding's theatrical mode, which focusses both on the inset performances and on "acting" as a metaphor for aspects of behaviour in the narrative as a whole, Irvin Ehrenpreis observes that the passionate lover called upon by Lady Bellaston is an act that Tom undertakes to play, and no more true to his identity than the role of bastard he has been playing all his life. The idea can be applied to Tom's entire performance as Lady Bellaston's "slave." He makes the appropriate heroic gestures, but his performance is deplorable, for it is not congruent with his basic decency—surely an essential ingredient in his character at all times. It is *not* the character of Tom to be "lascivious and effeminate," to borrow the words of Don Quixote lecturing Sancho Pancha on the subject of the Herculean hero. So in a very real sense Crane is right in claiming that "for the moment at least, a different Tom is before our eyes." This "difference," or, to be more precise, this discrepancy between character and assumed conduct, becomes the bearer of a major theme, inherent in the theatrical mode itself. Once again it is an aspect of *Tom Jones* which recalls *Don Quixote*. It is not, of course, life as performance, vision, dream that Fielding's novel approaches—not in any sense life in its existential aspects—but rather the relationship between mask and essence as a social and moral issue.

If Tom's affair with Lady Bellaston may be seen to consist in a series of heroic gestures, not necessarily appropriate to the character made to perform them, then it is fitting that it should begin as a *real* performance.

The masquerade highlights a distinction between those whose being merges with one particular social or moral role and those on whom the mask sits but uneasily. It will be remembered that Tom meets an anonymous lady at the masquerade, who makes her one and only appearance in that particular scene. She enters "in the Character of an old Woman" and is "one of those Ladies who go to a Masquerade only to vent Ill-nature." Her mask is synonymous with her being. Her only function is to mimic Lady Bellaston, whose real identity also merges with the mask—in fact, the mask defines her, specifically as an artificer of fraud. Their antithesis is Tom, whose mask is askance. He attempts to play a particular role, but does it badly. Ultimately the kind of heroic pose that is incongruent with the basic character of Tom connects with the moment when there is total divorce between gesture and character, between mask and essence. I am thinking of the imprisoned Tom at the beginning of book 18, as he is informed by Partridge that he has been to bed with the lady who is supposed to be his own mother. The horrified Partridge again assumes the posture of Hamlet, as he did during the performance of the play: just as "his Knees knocked against each other" while he was watching Garrick, he now appears before Tom "with his Face paler than Ashes, his Eyes fixed in his Head, his Hair standing an End, and every Limb trembling." Ghosts are less substantial in Fielding's world than in Shakespeare's—not, however, to Partridge, who "looked as he would have done had he seen a Spectre, or had he indeed been a Spectre himself." It is difficult not to think of Ophelia's famous description of Hamlet hard on the heels of his second encounter with the Ghost. What happens in Tom's cell is a repetition of the scene at the playhouse, when Partridge took part in the performance, imitating Garrick, and not knowing the distinction between a play acted and the particular world of which he is a part. In book 18, chapter 2, he transfers his posture to Tom, who believes he is guilty of incest with a mother, and makes all the frantic gestures of a hero in a Renaissance play. This time it is no longer a question of playing a part badly, but of making a series of totally empty gestures. However we define the substance of Tom and his actions, they bear no relationship at all to the theatrical pose assumed.

Theatricality may be a straightforward expression of hypocrisy and immorality, as for example in *Amelia,* or in *Sir Charles Grandison,* where masquerades serve as emblems of deceit pure and simple. In *Tom Jones* it is an all-pervasive mode, a few aspects of which this essay has attempted to approach. In a world consisting of parts acted, there are those that in the course of the narrative define themselves as empty and irrelevant, and those that are appropriate to the novel's social and moral geography. Some may be seen as both, depending on the system of logic and significance within which they are placed, and they may contradict *and* complement one another. Tom's performance in London, I hope to have shown, is one such case in point. Whatever the descriptive method, and whatever the interpretation arising from it, we are up against an art which ignores claims for an "organic," Jamesian interrelationship between character and incident. There are systems of coherence within the text that may potentially divide the element we call character. In some respects at least, the road from *Jonathan Wild* to *Tom Jones* may not be so long after all.

Fielding's Ecphrastic Moment: Tom Jones and His Egyptian Majesty

Manuel Schonhorn

Of all the digressions in Fielding's novels, none has generated more hesitant and indistinct commentary than the episode in *Tom Jones,* book 12, chapter 12, in which Tom and Partridge, lost in the woods near Coventry, discover a strange gypsy community presided over by an even stranger gypsy king. Let me only note that nearly every writer on Fielding before 1967 found nothing essential in the tale, or was confused by it, or disliked it, or dismissed it. That list includes George Sherburn, Irvin Ehrenpreis, Sheldon Sacks, Andrew Wright, and R. P. Mutter. From 1968 to the present, Charles Knight, J. Paul Hunter, Thomas Maresca, Douglas Brooks, and even Ronald Paulson, while gracefully vague, suggest that they subscribe to what we can call the digressive-disruptive-proleptic school of the earlier critics, or to the political reading given to the episode by Martin Battestin.

For it was in 1967 that Professor Battestin, in an influential *PMLA* article, published his reading of the adventure that is the most prevalent and the most acknowledged today. Building on a foundation of Egyptian history, contemporary political debate, and latitudinarian sermons supporting the Hanoverian monarchy, Professor Battestin concluded that the episode was an attack on Tory-Jacobite absolutism, an ironic parable of government, showing the dangers of one-man rule. Fielding, he wrote, is intent upon exposing the Jacobite ideal of civil happiness under an absolute ruler as nothing more than an alluring, but dangerous, fantasy.

From *Studies in Philology* 78, no. 3 (Summer 1981). © 1981 by Manuel Schonhorn.

Only two critics have disputed Professor Battestin's reading, and they have been virtually ignored. J. Lee Greene and Robert Folkenflik have written that within the context of the novel, the gypsy king is admirable and the gypsy episode presents an ideal political, civil, and social system.

It is not my purpose here to pursue in detail the weaknesses of these corrective voices, in their hunt for sources and in their continued judgments of the chapter's proleptic importance. And suggestions about the numerological, directional, and diagrammatical symbolism of the chapter, which would show that the episode is related to events antecedent to it, not subsequent to it, are best left to the notes. But since Odyssean parallels have been the stock in trade of Fielding explicators, it should be noted that book 12 of the *Odyssey* concludes with Odysseus's retrospective review of his wanderings to the Phaeacians, and book 13 is entitled, in the Pope text that Fielding knew best, "The Arrival of Ulysses in Ithaca." Fielding, in his book 13, entitles the final narrative movement of his Odyssean tale, "What befell Mr. Jones upon his Arrival in London." The importance of this echo from the *Odyssey* will be developed below.

I do not believe the purpose of book 12, chapter 12, lies in its anticipations or its political irony. Rather, it appears to me that Fielding has, in the gypsy king, brought before his reader a model of authority and order, the introduction to whom is a parody of earlier introductions to those less than satisfactory analogues of order, the Man of the Hill and the Master Puppeteer. And once again, Fielding has contrasted a golden age of artistic creation to the political realities of contemporary imperfections. To prove this, and to reveal the connections between book 12, chapter 12, and earlier events which it mimics and resolves, one must go beyond the coincidences already noted and take a closer look at Fielding's signalling language.

I

In book 8, chapter 10, Tom and Partridge, following a debate at a crossroads, lose their way on a cold, dark night.

> [Partridge's] chief Fear was that of Ghosts, with which the present Time of Night, and the Wildness of the Place extremely well suited.
> At this Instant *Partridge* espied a glimmering Light through

some Trees, which seemed very near to them . . . and both together made directly towards the Place whence the Light issued.

In spite of Partridge's fears, "whose Head was full of nothing but of Ghosts, Devils, Witches, and such like," Tom enters a neat and elegant cottage to confront an old crone, caretaker for its occupant. Such is the reader's ambiguous introduction to the Man of the Hill episode.

Four books later, in book 12, chapter 5, Tom and Partridge are "upon a wide Common where were several Roads." As before, Jones stopped "to consider which of these Roads he should pursue, when on a sudden they heard the Noise of a Drum that seemed at no great Distance. This Sound presently alarmed the Fears of *Partridge*," who believed them to be devils. But Jones, disregarding the advices of his companion "which Fear had inspired, made directly towards the Place whence the Noise proceeded," and coming "into a narrow Lane," discovers they are near an inn where a Master Puppeteer is to put on a show with puppets that are as big as life.

Now let us turn to the following gypsy chapter. Once again our travelers are lost in the dark, having missed the right road to Coventry.

> They now discovered a Light at some Distance, to the great Pleasure of *Jones,* and to the no small Terror of *Partridge,* who firmly believed himself to be bewitched, and that this Light was a *Jack with a Lantern,* or somewhat more mischievous.
>
> But how were these Fears increased, when, as they approached nearer to this Light, (or Lights as they now appeared) they heard a confused Sound of Human Voices; of singing, laughing, and hallowing, together with a strange Noise that seemed to proceed from some Instruments; but could hardly be allowed the Name of Music! Indeed, to favour a little the Opinion of *Partridge,* it might very well be called Music bewitched.

To Jones's correct surmise that they have come upon a "set of People who appear only to be merry-making," Partridge answers:

> "Merry-making, Sir . . . ! who could be merry-making at this Time of Night, and in such a Place, and such Weather? They can be nothing but Ghosts, or Witches, or some Evil Spirits, or other, that's certain."
>
> "Let them be what they will," cries *Jones,* "I am resolved

to go up to them, and enquire the Way to *Coventry.* All
Witches, *Partridge,* are not such ill-natured Hags as that we
had the Misfortune to meet with last."
 . . . At length they arrived at the Place whence the Lights
and different Noises had issued.

Such is the introduction to the paradoxical gypsy kingdom, with
Jones once again "a little surprized" at what he saw. The narrator's subsequent descriptions, supposedly rendered to reduce the comic terror of
the reader who has been expecting supernatural occurrences and hellish
personalities, is phrased in the language of the drama and the stage, "of
Managers and Playhouses," and "the Upper Gallery," I think to under-
score further the scene's similarity to the earlier digression at the inn,
where, it will be recalled, Tom debated with stupid playgoers the inertia
of moral comedy divested of the comic.

It thus seems to me that Fielding has deliberately contrived book 12,
chapter 12 to be read as a redaction or conflation of those two earlier
adventures. What binds them is that they have all introduced anticipated
and expected orderers of life and art—in the two earlier examples a supposedly wise and benevolent Man of the Hill and a creatively knowl-
edgeable Master Puppeteer. But both have been revealed to be false and
dangerous threats to harmony, disrupters of both existential and aesthetic
truths. The forms of their art—a deceiving picaresque narrative and a
flawed puppet entertainment—are obviously negative paradigms of the
kind of dramatic illusion and the correct authorial posture exhibited in
Fielding's novel. The confusion between reality and illusion, life and art,
is manifest in both their performances. In neither is there an on-stage
intelligence to evaluate and do justice to the moment in which their art
and experience have placed them. Surprisingly, the gypsy king develops
as an unexpected refutation of those previous ironic paragons. Initially,
he resembles but immediately diverges from those false surrogates of
order and value. Henry Knight Miller, in his study of the romance back-
grounds to Fielding's tales, has remarked that "one of the added pleasures
of a tradition in which certain elements are self-justifying because part
of an expected pattern of gestalt, is that not only do variations and in-
terpolations provide freshness and surprise, but also any change in the
pattern is immediately felt as significant, because one has a pattern to
measure significant variation by." He and others have helped us to understand Fielding better through the perspective of romance traditions,
which Fielding parodically inverts for serious and comic effect. What I

would here suggest is that we can come to read Fielding with as much insight through the perspective of Fielding. A characteristic pattern of his art is the arousal of the reader's expectations with a sequential pattern of his own creation, and the comic reversal of that response.

But book 12, chapter 12, contains a more important pattern and conflation of earlier actions whose consequences have been overlooked by all. Let me continue with the nature of ecphrasis and its relation to Fielding's novel. My final reading of the gypsy king adventure, I hope, will be something *more* than, to quote Earl Wasserman, "a creative activity by the reader who is invited by an allusion to exercise his own invention, by contemplating the relevance of the entire allusive context."

II

Fielding's allusive tag by which he introduces his hero and the reader to the strange community of the gypsies and to the narrative activity that provokes the judgments of the gypsy king recalls one of the best-known ecphrases in Western literature, imitated by Renaissance poets and explicated by all Renaissance critics and mythographers:

Dum stupet obtutuque haeret defixus in uno.

Maurice Johnson many years ago cautioned us about Fielding's untranslated classical quotations seen in obviously significant contexts. Except for Partridge's commonplace and generally silly Latin mottoes drawn from Lily's *Grammar,* Fielding's school text, this is one of the very few Latin quotations left untranslated, and the mystery is further compounded by its centrality on the printed page.

Dryden's translation is: "Thus while the Trojan prince employs his eyes, / Fixed on the walls with wonder and surprise." The quotation is from book 1 of the *Aeneid,* in which Aeneas enters Dido's city and sees on the temple walls the handicraft of several artists depicting scenes from the Trojan War.

Ecphrasis was the exercise in description designed to train classical students in vivid presentation of details. It taught them to describe graphically and to display particulars to the eyes of the mind. Following the language and examples of his predecessors, Hermogones, in the second century, explains: "An ecphrasis is an account in detail, visible, as they say, bringing before one's eyes what is to be shown. Ecphrases are of persons, actions, times, places, seasons, and many other things." From this beginning it developed into the special genre by which we know it today, the poetical description of an art object, or the art object within the art object.

But once again the classical handbooks reveal that critical commentary lagged behind creative practice, and from ecphrasis's earliest use rhetorical structure failed to explain aesthetic function. For example, look at Homer's ecphrasis that served as a kind of model for subsequent poets, the shield of Achilles in book 18 of the *Iliad*. Pope's notes to his translation of Homer tell us more about the purpose of the ecphrasis than do the rhetoricians, and permit us to see how it was understood by Fielding's contemporaries: "Homer's Intention was no less, than to draw the Picture of the whole World in the Compass of this Shield. We see first the Universe in general; the Heavens are spread, the Stars are hung up, the Earth is stretched forth, the Seas are pour'd round: We next see the World in a nearer and more particular view; the Cities, delightful in Peace, or formidable in War; the Labours of the Countrey, and the Fruit of those Labours, in the Harvests and the Vintages; the Pastoral Life in its Pleasures and its Dangers: In a Word, all the Occupations, all the Ambitions, and all the Diversions of Mankind." For Pope, Homer's ecphrasis is more than a digressive description. On the one hand, the shield serves as a symbol of the poem itself, widening the "perspective of the poem, universalizing its visionary scope." His glosses also suggest that the shield enables the poet to bring to the reader a world that the battle narrative itself could not absorb. The shield serves as a total construct of the world outside the text. Ecphrasis thus enabled the poet to harmonize his work, to transcend the limits of the poem's reality. As it was to be developed into the Renaissance, one can say that the poet had introduced into the actuality of his art a structured, more complete, and fully resolved fiction which coalesced with the poem's limited narrative activity.

Virgil, Pope writes, "was charm'd with *Achilles*'s Shield, and therefore would give the same Ornament to his Poem. But as *Homer* had painted the Universe, he was sensible that nothing remain'd for him to do; he had no other way to take than that of Prophecy, and shew what the Descendant of his Hero should perform." Pope thus understood how, in his account of Aeneas's shield, Virgil developed a feature of ecphrasis that was to prove influential in the epic poetry of the Renaissance. As George Kurman writes, "[Virgil] used the shield to represent the past history of a people, or from the point of view of narrative time, to convey what can be termed 'apparent prophecy.' Virgil purports to portray the future, to show events posterior to the present of the narrative. . . . The use of ecphrases in the three most important Renaissance epics in the

Romance tongues [Ariosto's, Camoens's, and Tasso's] shows that this device had become an integral part of epic style." Further, Pope reveals the age's recognition of the imaginative adaptation of the ecphrastic conventions of Homer and Virgil when he moves from his commentary on Achilles' shield to quote at length Milton's lines in the eleventh book, the prophetic book, of *Paradise Lost,* as Michael unfolds for Adam mankind's future: "I ought not to forget the many apparent Allusions to the Descriptions on this Shield, which are to be found in those Pictures of Peace and War, the City and the Countrey, in the eleventh Book of *Milton*: Who was doubtless fond of any Occasion to shew, how much he was charm'd with the Beauty of all these lively Images. He makes his Angel paint those Objects which he shews to *Adam,* in the Colours, and almost the very Strokes of *Homer.*"

But if ecphrasis could be used to harmonize or resolve the main narrative, or to amplify or simply paradigmatically parallel it, it also enabled the poet to do some historical tidying up, so to speak, to take the narrative beyond its fictive present by anticipating a foreshadowed end. In Shakespeare's *Rape of Lucrece,* for example, the ecphrasis is of the identical scene that arrests Aeneas's attention in Dido's temple. Lucrece stands in mediation before a tapestry showing the destruction of Troy. Here not only are the themes of Shakespeare's poem illuminated by this view of them in a different context; not only can the life of the literary work be interpreted in terms of the ecphrastic—or art—object; in addition, the reader is led to observe the similarities of fates which the rape of Helen brought upon the denizens of Priam's world and Tarquin's action brought upon the Tarquinians. Shakespeare's ecphrasis permits the rape action to be played out to its Roman end. Like its source, Shakespeare's ecphrasis is an artistic model which the poem itself only partially fulfills.

In addition, in an important modification which no doubt has been noticed, ecphrasis had become something more than the examples given by the rhetoricians: seasons, persons, a description of a battle that took place at night, or a description of the Acropolis at Alexandria; it had now become the conscious projection of an earlier creation of art. That is, where Homer's shield refracted the whole world beyond the actions of the *Iliad,* Virgil represents Dido's friezes in terms of remembered scenes from Homer's epic, Homer's art; and Shakespeare's ecphrasis is a free development of Virgil's Roman story, Virgil's art.

One final observation has to be made. Fielding's tag, Aeneas's vision of Carthage's walls, carry the reader back to what has long been rec-

ognized as the source for Virgil's scene, to that memorable account in
the *Odyssey* which anticipates Odysseus's revelation of his identity to his
Phaeacian hosts. The blind bard, Demodocus—who, Pope reminds us,
had been generally thought to be Homer himself—had earlier in the book
sung of Odysseus's victories in the war. Now, Odysseus asks of the bard,

> Once more harmonious strike the sounding string,
> Th' Epaean fabric, fram'd by *Pallas,* sing:
> How stern *Ulysses,* furious to destroy,
> With latent heroes sack'd imperial *Troy.*

Demodocus complies and sings, "How [Odysseus] attends, / . . . and
how with dire alarms / He fights, subdues: for *Pallas* strings his arms."
Odysseus weeps, as Aeneas later wept, in Rolfe Humphries's haunting
phrase, at those stilled monuments of the wars whose fame had travelled
the whole world over.

What is the persistent pattern in all the ecphrases allusively echoing
in Fielding's text now becomes clearer: in one way or another, our dramatic characters, even Milton's Adam, I shall suggest in a moment, adrift
in the uncertainty of a fictional life, hear of or see themselves as figures
in art. Odysseus sobs to hear of his epic self; Aeneas weeps as "Himself
he saw, amidst the Grecian train"; Lucrece projects in her tears her tragic
recognition of her violated self as she identifies with both Hecuba and
Troy; and even Milton's Adam, ready to listen to the future glories of
his race, ascends a hill that, in Milton's words, "for different cause the
Tempter set / Our second Adam, in the wilderness." Not only have the
ecphrases been the foci of their situations; they have almost always revealed to them, but always to us, some other self that glorifies them with
the permanence of immortality, for they have been "distilled and formed
into the pure permanence of art." Like Don Quixote, as these archetypical
heroes and heroine of Western civilization pursue their divergent adventures on their roads of life, they all seem to have become "heroes of
literature during their own lifetime"; that is, they all meet themselves on
that journey fused into the permanence of art.

What I have here presented should now make my reading of book 12,
chapter 12, transparent. Fielding's text has given the signals so long overlooked: Tom, too, has journeyed into a picture, which, if unseen and
misunderstood by him, should not have been by us. He has confronted
himself. Fielding's ecphrastic moment has become his commentary on
his composition.

The History of Tom Jones, A Foundling began with a bill of fare to the feast within it; it ends with a festive supper and a wedding, three in fact. "There have not," the narrator remarks in his conclusion, "been many Instances of a Number of People met together, where every one was so perfectly happy, as in this Company. . . . The Evening was spent in much true Mirth. All were happy, but those the most, who had been most unhappy before." Squire Western, irrepressible as ever with the visions of grandchildren dancing in his head, "was soon reduced to Order. Notwithstanding this little Restraint, he was . . . pleased with the Chearfulness and Good-Humour of the Company." But earlier in book 12, chapter 12, we had met with another company, "now celebrating the Wedding of one of their Society." There too:

> It is impossible to conceive a happier Set of People than appeared here to be met together. The utmost Mirth indeed shewed itself in every Countenance; nor was their Ball totally void of all Order and Decorum. Perhaps it had more than a Country Assembly is sometimes conducted with: For these People are subject to a formal Government and Laws of their own, and all pay Obedience to one great Magistrate, whom they call their King.
>
> Greater Plenty likewise was no where to be seen, than what flourished in this Barn. Here was indeed no Nicety nor Elegance, nor did the keen Appetite of the Guests require any. Here was good Store of Bacon, Fowls, and Mutton, to which every one present provided better Sauce himself, than the best and dearest *French* Cook can prepare.

In my view, Fielding has constructed book 12, chapter 12, as an epitome of the great world that surrounds it, an episode of ironically "low" art that is a microcosm of his whole narrative context. For is not book 12, chapter 12, made up of actions, accusations, evidences, witnesses, and the execution of a true sentence—one of the rarest in the whole book—which we have applauded along with Tom? In a word, Justice? And has this not been the prevailing metaphor of Fielding's fiction? When the gypsy king upbraids and punishes the gypsy couple for their unnatural sexual behavior, and does not even mention or indict Partridge for his "natural" behavior, does this not argue for the narrator's—and our—judgment of Tom for his sexual behavior anticipated at the novel's end? Even the gypsy king's packing the criminals off in shame resembles the narrator's exile and rejection of Blifil and Lady Bellaston, who, as Professor Ehrenpreis has remarked, "are the only two characters Fielding does not seem to be able to sympathize with."

Book 12, chapter 12, it seems to me, has been misinterpreted or misread all these years because we have ignored the action that is its dramatic center, that gives to the chapter its significance, and that finally provokes the Solomon-like judgment of the gypsy king, which is clearly supported by Tom and the narrator. I mean Partridge's seduction by the gypsy wife.

> A sudden Uproar arose in the Barn, and as it seems upon this Occasion: The Courtesy of these People had by degrees removed all the Apprehensions of *Partridge,* and he was prevailed upon not only to stuff himself with their Food, but to taste some of their Liquors, which by degrees entirely expelled all Fear from his Composition, and in its Stead introduced much more agreeable Sensations.
>
> A young Female *Gypsy,* more remarkable for her Wit than her Beauty, had decoyed the honest Fellow aside, pretending to tell his Fortune. Now when they were alone together in a remote part of the Barn, whether it proceeded from the strong Liquor, which is never so apt to inflame inordinate Desire as after moderate Fatigue; or whether the fair Gypsy herself threw aside the Delicacy and Decency of her Sex, and tempted the Youth *Partridge* with express Solicitations; but they were discovered in a very improper Manner by the Husband of the *Gypsy.*

It seems reasonable to argue that every word, every nuance, every image, calling up every memory of our reading, reveals this scene to be a conflation of the two previous scenes in which the youth Tom had been tempted and seduced by Molly Seagrim and Jenny Waters. Lubricious and lascivious, Partridge has been stuffed with food and drink, as Jones earlier had been. For he had been literally drunk when he retired into the bushes with Molly Seagrim. And Molly, though "generally thought a very fine Girl, . . . yet her Beauty was not of the most amiable Kind. It had indeed very little of the Feminine in it, and would have become a Man at least as well as a Woman; for, to say the Truth, Youth and florid Health had a very considerable Share in the Composition." Drunken Jones and his "fair Hind," you will remember, were later discovered in a very improper manner by the perambulating Thwackum and Blifil.

In like manner, several books later, Jenny Jones, with a face that had not "much Appearance of Beauty," also lures young Tom into an assignation at Upton. There, vast pieces of beef and bottled ale helped to break down the resistance of our young hero to the "fair Warrior," "the Fair one." "In short, no sooner had the amorous Parley ended, and the Lady had unmasked the Royal Battery, by carelessly letting her Handkerchief drop from her Neck, than the Heart of Mr. *Jones* was entirely taken, and the fair Conqueror enjoyed the usual Fruits of her Victory." Later, as we would expect, Jones and his fair one are discovered by the Irishman Fitzpatrick stalking his runaway wife.

In both cases, the narrator has made it very clear that youthful Tom has been tempted by and succumbed to the blandishments of the fair sex. I think we are asked to see in book 12, chapter 12—even if Tom cannot— our hero coming upon his parodic self, in an act which defines his peculiar nature and has determined his wanderings as much as the valor and piety of Odysseus and Aeneas have determined theirs. And once again, I suspect that our inability to read this scene as the narrator wished us to read it has been a consequence of the realism we have been taught to expect and even demand of what purports to be a historical fiction. For the narrator's description of "the Youth Partridge" should never have served for glosses of the following kind: "he of course is now over fifty," implying another factual lapse on Fielding's part.

Immediately before book 12, chapter 12, the narrator had gone out of his way to remind us that Tom's fellow traveler was "now a middle-aged Man." And only seven or so pages after book 12, chapter 12, in an action almost constructed to force the sense of the disparity of their ages upon us, the narrator again went out of his way to create a dispute between Tom and Partridge over Latin declensions. As far as I can see, the sole purpose of the latter scene is to have Tom provoked by a man of years and to call him "a conceited old Fool," and "an old Rogue," and for Partridge to assert the disrespect of his "young Gentleman." All this language, it must be noted, was never touched or revised in any way when Fielding made those extensive revisions in the third and fourth editions of the novel.

And finally, what of Tom Jones's Egyptian majesty? Fielding, I believe, has asked us to regard this venerable person who approaches us "with many friendly Salutations, rather of too hearty a Kind to be called courtly," who "was very little distinguished in Dress from his Subjects, nor had he any *Regalia* of Majesty to support his Dignity; and yet there seemed (as Mr. *Jones* said) to be somewhat in his Air which denoted Authority and inspired the Beholders with an Idea of Awe and Respect"—

Fielding has determined that we regard him as the dramatic version of the narrator himself.

A *pater patriae* of "as orderly and well governed People as any upon Face of de Earth." A king and monarch who "can boast of no more dutiful Subject, ne no more affectionate." A majesty who "never design any Ting but to do dem Good. For what can me do oderwise dan consider of de Good of dose poor People who go about all Day to give me always the best of what dey got. Dey love and honour me darefor, because me do love and take care of dem." Who made "all his Subject equal vid each oder," and who assures us "it be ver troublesome ting to be King, and always to do Justice."

Who can this be if not our narrator, whom we have been listening to throughout in the larger tale of his own creation? For, far from maintaining a divine distance from his story, as one critic has strangely written, Fielding's narrator has from the book's inception been the moral and legal center of his storied world. Without him, we would be witnessing a chaotic universe, superintended by a sterile Allworthy, a concupiscent Bridget, brutal schoolmasters, muddleheaded philosophers, lawyers, doctors, innkeepers, barbers, and an assortment of servants right out of Jonson's comedies. Without the gypsy king, we would be confronting, to use the language Professor Battestin has hypnotized us with to assert the spurious moral order which he thinks they represent—"an alien band of itinerant fortune tellers and thieves," "rogues," "beggars," and a herd of "robbers"—only fit to alarm and make anxious the citizens of Austen's Highbury.

Both narrator and gypsy king are the controlling intelligences of their worlds, factual and fictional, historical and pastoral. Both narrator and gypsy king dominate and contain their respective communities with an antique grace and an astounding tolerance for the creatures they oversee. Their subjects too—factual and fictional, historical and pastoral—are all wanderers over the English landscape, and it is among these that they both stay chaos and assert order and justice. And our narrator and king have both carried us to the end of their episodes, to pseudo-catastrophes, which bring about the right distribution of rewards and punishments and restore a natural and moral harmony in their communities.

Much work still remains to be done that will help us to understand and appreciate more the complexity of Fielding's chapter. Here I can only ask the reader to recall the paternal fondness and authorial dignity both monarchs share. Throughout his book, the narrator's compassion, friendship, and love for his actors on his stage—his children he has called them—has paralleled his comic enjoyment of their travails. It is enough to cite one early confession of that imperious yet benevolent judge, legislator, and deity, who has always been on his platform, in Professor Booth's phrase, "to remind us, through his wisdom and benevolence, of what human life ought to be and might be," that narrator whom we must see in harmony with the most important norms of the gypsy king:

> For as I am, in reality, the Founder of a new Province of Writing, so I am at liberty to make what Laws, I please therein. And these laws, my Readers, whom I consider as my Subjects, are bound to believe in and to obey; with which that they may readily and chearfully comply, I do hereby assure them, that I shall principally regard their Ease and Advantage in all such Institutions. For I do not, like a *jure divino* Tyrant, imagine that they are my Slaves, or my Commodity. I am, indeed, set over them for their own Good only, and was created for their Use, and not they for mine. Nor do I doubt, while I make their Interest the great Rule of my Writings, they will unanimously concur in supporting my Dignity, and in rendering me all the Honour I shall deserve or desire.

The narrator's farewell to his reader, strangely enough in the stagecoach metaphor that had been used earlier to denigrate apology-writing historians, might explain why this paean to the self as artist, and to his work, rooted within the pages of his own creation, was necessary. Histories must end; the balloons of fiction must burst; and the unconsecrated host of our entertainment must give way to the more substantial fictions of experience. But Fielding's art remains, purged of finitude and unfixity in a golden world of ecphrastic perfection. Justice and Kingship remain, beyond the insecure, because temporal and historical, resolutions of the fiction. *The History of Tom Jones,* which is only an aesthetic entertainment, will pass; the fiction of the gypsy king fixed in the pastoral and immutable world of purer art, will endure. The transient values of the host's creation—the novel *Tom Jones*—will continue to thrive in an utopian kingdom where the ideals of justice, freedom, and a golden age of abundance and equality prevail.

III

The seemingly irreconcilable contradictions between Professor Battestin's reading of book 12, chapter 12—"a quaint, ironic image of uto-

pia," "a world, in other words, not attainable at all except, perhaps, in
the nostaligic fantasies of Tory squires"—and the one argued above
should not depress us into attributing a Gödel-like paradox to Fielding's
literary creation. Within the text, with the insistent and more than co-
incidental parallels to similar episodes elsewhere in the book, and with
the sympathy with which the narrator portrays the gypsies, the episode
suggests a world of art. And within this fictive world, human passions,
misdirections, and myopia are as real as they are in life, but it is the
moral commitment, ethical perception and wisdom of the artist that
defeats them, to render the fiction eternal. Surely the voice of the narrator
has also clearly told us that political absolutism remains, but such meaning is clearly external to and divorced from the narrative itself. But also
surely Fielding has immediately and obviously passed from the world of
the fiction to the fact of England in 1745, the latter introduced with a
voice that is separated in tone and time from the completed action within
the gypsy domain. No reader until the present time has mistaken that
abrupt transition, and no reader can mistake Fielding's momentary vision, attenuated perhaps as we recall the strength and security of Pope's,
of enduring and superior art's victory over transiency and temporality.
In book 12, chapter 12, contrast, not collusive ambiguity or irony, is at
work; a world of art versus parochial truths of history. Thus to move
events of the created, ordered, and beautifully articulated world of *Tom
Jones* so crudely into the reader's England is to undermine all we know
about Fielding's delicate analogical art.

Much of the best of Fielding scholarship has made clear the pervasive
manner in which Fielding, in his fictions, created a tension or established
a commentary by juxtaposing the literary and the living as counterparts.
But rather than resolving the rivalry between the "real" world of the
novel and the more formal generic representations of art eased into it,
more often than not these representations or digressions point up the
contrast between a fictional ideality and the imperfect actualities of life,
political or otherwise. For example, in *Joseph Andrews,* there is perhaps
an earlier and cruder exemplification of the pattern dramatized in
book 12, chapter 12, of *Tom Jones*. Mr. Wilson, the obvious moral ex-
emplar of that fiction, introduces a self-conscious and serious digression
about the London world from which he has escaped to a pastoral paradise,
which, in its domestic order and rural harmony, anticipates much of the
ambience of the gypsy king's terrain. Mr. Wilson's interpretive acumen
is equal to the gypsy king's; his supervision of joy and social content
also is equal to that of the later monarch. But here too the Golden World

of digressive retrospection is upset by an intrusive action, violent and disruptive, in the midst of Mr. Wilson's ordered pastoral paradise. The accident here is the wanton murder of the eldest daughter's little dog by the son of the lord of the manor, "as absolute as any tyrant in the universe."

Parson Adams's departing comment, "that this was the manner in which the people lived in the Golden Age," has generally been taken as a comic example of his naiveté and quixotic perception of an oft-times imperfect world. And so it is. But the element of real insight in Adams's evaluation should not be overlooked. Among the many serious services Mr. Wilson's digression performs in *Joseph Andrews* that are analogous to those performed in the gypsy interlude of *Tom Jones,* one surely is its relative opposition of a world of fictional art and the world of the novel. Fielding's paragon remarked then that "no blessings are pure in this world," yet Fielding appears to permit him to tell us, what the gypsy king has told and what the narrator has been telling us, that the golden age of art hooked out of the narrative momentum of the larger fiction surrounding it, presents the only testament to the possibility of insight and order.

Tom Jones and the Farewell to Providential Fiction

Leopold Damrosch, Jr.

Character and Desire

The greatest single literary work of the eighteenth century is Fielding's *Tom Jones* (1749), that urbane and spacious fable in which pragmatic knowledge of the world is made to harmonize with gratified desire. An omniscient and affectionate narrator acts as the disposing deity of the fictional universe, instructing the reader, by means of a plot whose coherence is only gradually revealed, to understand the operations of a Providence that subsumes all of the apparent accidents of chance or Fortune. *Tom Jones* thus triumphantly unites philosophical meaning with fictive form, in ways that stand in a fascinating relation with the Puritan tradition we have been surveying. At the deepest level Fielding is in harmony with it, believing not only that life is providentially ordered (most novelists for the next century and a half believed that) but also that the shape of a fictional work can directly imitate that order. But in many ways he is unsympathetic to Puritan narrative, which indeed served as a negative stimulus when he left playwriting for fiction (*Joseph Andrews* began as a burlesque of Richardson's *Pamela*). I propose to survey two of the central themes of the present book—the idea of the self (or personality, or character), and the relation between human mimesis and God's plot—as a way of seeing the Puritan tradition in perspective while

From *God's Plot and Man's Stories: Studies in the Fictional Imagination from Milton to Fielding*. © 1985 by the University of Chicago. University of Chicago Press, 1985.

recognizing the precariousness, by the middle of the eighteenth century, of any art that claimed to unite formal principles with philosophical ones.

In Fielding's narratives, unlike those we have been considering thus far, mimesis is the work of a highly visible artist who selects and shapes the materials that life affords, in an ambiguous union of Aristotelian generalization with Platonic idealization, transforming (as Sidney said in the *Apology*) nature's brazen world into a golden one. Preoccupied with the embattled state of the self in a fallen world, Puritan narrative is often grim and always potentially tragic. Augustan narrative, even in dark satires like *Gulliver's Travels* and Pope's *Dunciad,* is often playful and always potentially comic. (I use the word "Augustan" as a convenient term for writers in the classical humanist tradition who admired the cultural values, if not the politics, of Augustan Rome.)

The absence of humor might almost provide a litmus test for identifying Puritan writing. Joan Webber, who notes that even on his deathbed Donne "puns as if his life depended on it," suggests that the Puritan avoids humor because "to the extent that art is play, he finds it hard to accept, and he often sees the conservative as someone who plays with words, because he cannot believe that such play may be serious." We remember Bunyan's solemn declaration of veracity:

> I could have stepped into a style much higher than this in which I have here discoursed, and could have adorned all things more than here I have seemed to do: but I dare not: God did not play in convincing of me; the Devil did not play in tempting of me; neither did I play when I sunk as into a bottomless pit, when *the pangs of hell caught hold upon me:* wherefore I may not play in my relating of them, but be plain and simple, and lay down the thing as it was.

The Puritan fear of play—both verbal wit and fictive invention—reflects a deep commitment to reading God's story rather than substituting one's own, but it also reflects a fear that the self might find freedom in play. Humor, as Erikson says of Luther's willingness to joke, "marks the moment when our ego regains some territory from oppressive conscience." But Puritans were generally committed to the belief that conscience ought to be the ego's constant authority and guide. Lovelace jests constantly, Clarissa never, and although there is some grim wit in *Paradise Lost,* a Miltonic joke is no laughing matter. Dickens called *Robinson Crusoe* "the only instance of an universally popular book that could make no one laugh and could make no one cry." Fielding and Richardson seem to have divided the alternatives between them.

Not all wit is affirming, of course. Hobbes's account of laughter as "sudden glory" at another's expense is disturbingly apt to Augustan satire, and in Pope—not to speak of Swift, who was never seen to laugh—there is always an edge of bitterness and scorn. Fielding had plenty of disappointed bitterness in his life, but *Tom Jones* stands immortally as a supremely Apollonian invention, sunlit and serene, in which evil is mastered, Dionysian energies harmonized, and the self liberated to fulfill its own best impulses. Seeing man as embattled amid fearful dangers, Puritan fiction was drawn to the image of the prison: Christian in Doubting Castle and Vanity Fair, Crusoe on his island, Clarissa in her locked rooms. For Fielding the central image is the road, that scene of unpredictable openness in picaresque fiction which he transforms into a confirmation that we should keep moving, onward not inward, until we get to a happy ending. At the end of *Tom Jones* he describes his narrative as a "long journey." In a narrow sense this is a plot device, since the road permits Tom to meet the people who can rescue him from undeserved disgrace, but more than that it is a fundamental principle of affirmation, life seen as possibility rather than as threat.

Puritan fiction was born of the individual's quest for a counter-*nomos,* Augustan fiction of the need to restore the old *nomos* and protect it from the unpredictableness of the separate individual. In the search for truth, Dryden wrote, we do well to curb our private notions if they threaten to disturb public peace, for "common quiet is mankind's concern." Dryden was a relentless satirist of Puritan individualism, and like Pope and Swift after him he supported the social hierarchy which Puritanism was committed to extirpating. If all men are radically corrupt, then as Haller says "the absolute levels all relatives; all men are born equal." Fielding knows that many of the rich and powerful are unworthy of their position, but all the same he believes in an aristocracy of goodness that overlaps to some extent with social status.

Allworthy is modeled on the philanthropist Ralph Allen of Bath, whom Pope also eulogized, in accordance with a social ethic that encourages the prosperous to integrate their inferiors into a comfortable *nomos.*

> His house is not quite a mile from this place. . . . There, I
> say, thou mayest be eased of thy burden, and if thou art not
> minded to go back to thy former habitation, as indeed I would

not wish thee, thou mayest send for thy wife and children to
thee to this village, where there are houses [that] now stand
empty, one of which thou mayest have at reasonable rates;
provision is there also cheap and good, and that which will
make thy life the more happy is, to be sure there thou shalt
live by honest neighbours, in credit and good fashion.

This idyllic proposal would not be out of place in *Tom Jones,* but it is in
fact an account of Mr. Legality as delivered by Worldly-Wiseman. Fielding of course abhors hypocrisy and regularly satirizes worldliness, but
there is no denying that he would be at home in the village of Morality,
as is apparent in his frequent denunciations of sects like the Methodists
that favor faith over works. In Kierkegaard's terms he is ethical whereas
the Puritans were religious, and celebrates the sympathy that unites the
group rather than the existential leap that isolates the rare individual:

The knight of faith is obliged to rely upon himself alone, he
feels the pain of not being able to make himself intelligible to
others, but he feels no vain desire to guide others. . . . The
true knight of faith is a witness, never a teacher, and therein
lies his deep humanity, which is worth a good deal more than
this silly participation in others' weal and woe which is hon-
ored by the name of sympathy, whereas in fact it is nothing
but vanity.

Fielding would find this formulation inexplicable if not diabolical. In *Tom
Jones* he satirizes something very like it in the misanthropic hermit the
Man of the Hill.

For all its criticism of specific abuses, *Tom Jones* is deeply committed
to ratifying the social order, and is thus a "double theodicy" of the kind
Weber and Berger describe, providing the poor with an explanation of
their poverty and the rich with an explanation of their wealth. "The
result is one of world-maintenance and, very concretely, of the maintenance of the particular institutional order." Society is the vast structure
into which one happens to be born, rather than a special subgroup vol-
untarily entered by the elect, and one's place in it is confirmed by one's
nature and one's actions together. Blifil is the legitimate son of Bridget
Allworthy, Tom the illegitimate son, but Tom deserves to live at Paradise
Hall while the vicious Blifil must be ejected from it. It is a question both
of deserving and of choosing to fit in, as Locke indicates with (very
likely) a backward glance at the Puritans: "He must be of a strange and

unusual constitution, who can content himself to live in constant disgrace and disrepute with his own particular society."

This social orientation governs the conception of character. It is no longer a question of the unique individual confronting an alien world, but rather of the typical character developing in accordance with the pressures of a particular time and place. Puritan autobiographers sought to find conventional patterns in their lives just because they felt their individuality so keenly, and the Calvinist tradition leads directly to Rousseau with his boast that nature broke the mold after forming him. The Augustan attitude is closer to S. J. Perelman's: "Before they made me they broke the mold." All men are defective, but that is a familiar fact of the human condition, not an occasion for obsessive self-hatred. And whereas the Puritan individual must learn like Clarissa to strip away all ties of family and society, the Augustan individual grows freely, like a living plant, under the influence of the multiple relationships that Locke describes: "One single man may at once be concerned in, and sustain all these following relations, and many more, viz. father, brother, son, grandfather, grandson, father-in-law, son-in-law, husband, friend, enemy, subject, general, judge, patron, client, professor, European, Englishman, islander, servant, master, possessor, captain, superior, inferior, bigger, less, older, younger, contemporary, like, unlike, etc., to an almost infinite number." Tom Jones is neither an isolated soul nor a human being in the abstract; he is Bridget's son, Allworthy's nephew, Blifil's half-brother, Sophia's lover, Partridge's friend, and so on. One function of the plot of *Tom Jones* is to dispel false versions of these relationships while demonstrating that the true ones are congruent with Tom's essential character.

The idea of an interior and mysterious self has little relevance for Fielding, whose neoclassical conception of character assumes that the people we meet in life are in fact types. As he says in *Joseph Andrews*, contrasting his fiction with the "romances" of ostensibly objective historians,

> I declare here once for all, I describe not men, but manners; not an individual, but a species. Perhaps it will be answered, Are not the characters then taken from life? To which I answer in the affirmative; nay, I believe I might aver, that I have writ little more than I have seen. The lawyer is not only alive, but hath been so these 4000 years.

What is wanted is not mimicry but verisimilitude, as Fielding comments in *Tom Jones:*

> Vanbrugh and Congreve copied nature; but they who copy
> them draw as unlike the present age, as Hogarth would do if
> he was to paint a rout or a drum [i.e., fashionable parties] in
> the dresses of Titian and of Vandyke. In short, imitation here
> will not do the business. The picture must be after nature
> herself.

Types are not stereotypes, since the type will always be shaped and specialized by the details of time and place, but individuality is not individualism. Rather than postulating a unique and hidden consciousness at the heart of the self, Fielding sees character as the sum of visible actions and decisions. If these sometimes remain hidden, that is only because a mask has successfully concealed them, not because they lurk in a deep and torchlit cavern. Moreover, one does not enter the world with a fully realized self, but instead one gradually builds up and revises it, as is described in the autobiographical writings of Hume, Gibbon, and Franklin.

Whereas the Puritans defined unwanted impulses as no part of the self, or at least as ebullitions from a lower and contemptible part, Fielding is interested in the whole person and sees even the oddest behavior as expressive of a person's real nature. This is the tradition that leads to Dickens, the comic or satiric vision that interprets quirks of character as deeply chosen self-caricature—Wemmick with his postbox grin, Jaggers's compulsive hand-washing. For as Ferenczi remarks, "Character is from the point of view of the psychoanalyst a sort of abnormality, a kind of mechanization of a particular way of reaction, rather similar to an obsessional symptom." When an apparently simple type-character in Fielding suddenly reveals "human" complications, for example when the philosopher Square is discovered undressed in Molly Seagrim's bedroom, the point is not that Fielding has switched literary modes but rather that an unpredictable aspect of a character is suddenly revealed. Motives are additive in Fielding's world, sometimes visible at a glance, sometimes revealed over a period of time, sometimes hidden forever. But they are never *necessarily* hidden: it is a question of what one happens to find out, not of intrinsic limitations upon knowing. In Richardson's world, motives are obscure and disturbing, not a collection but an abyss.

Just as motive is unmysterious, so the behavior of good characters like Tom and Sophia is instinctively right, directed by what Fielding repeatedly calls "Good Nature." For a Puritan there can be no such thing as good nature. Nature is the enemy, to be combatted by grace. Fielding's outward-looking, benevolist ethic is at the farthest remove from Puritan soul-searching, as is his tendency to excuse Tom's blunders because his heart is good. We remember the bitterness with which Clarissa learns the duplicities of her heart, and the misplaced confidence with which the doomed Lovelace boasts that he himself is "honest" and "ingenuous." Tom Jones may not always know exactly what his real motives are, but his heart is in the right place. For persons possessed of Good Nature, sentiment or feeling becomes a guide to conduct, whereas Puritans like Bunyan feared it as a villainous tempter: "There was, moreover, one Mr. Feeling; but he was no captain, but a great stickler to encourage Mansoul to rebellion."

Johnson wrote tartly in a sermon, "There is no topic more the favorite of the present age, than the innocence of error accompanied with sincerity." It is no wonder that hypocrisy was so central a theme in the fiction of his contemporaries, for if moral feeling has instinctive goodness as its inner form, it has sincerity as its outward sign, and this is easily imitated. Lovelace's role-playing is in effect normal in a culture that sees itself in dramatic terms and likes to peer, as Fielding puts it in *Tom Jones,* "behind the scenes of this greater theater of Nature." Tom is sincere while Blifil only seems sincere, but even the judicious Allworthy gets the two confused. No doubt inspired by the Tom/Blifil contrast, Sheridan found the perfect theatrical analogue, the fallen screen in *The School for Scandal* that exposes the villainy of Joseph Surface and vindicates his worthy brother Charles. The part of Joseph Surface was written expressly for John Palmer, an actor popularly known as Plausible Jack. Palmer later seceded from Sheridan's company, fell on hard times, and tried to return; when he protested "If you could but see my heart, Mr. Sheridan," the playwright replied, "Why, Jack, you forget I wrote it."

However shrewdly the comic writers see through hypocrisy, they persist in regarding it as an aberration that can be detected and put to rout. What they will not concede is the full pessimism of a position like Pascal's:

> Man is nothing but disguise, lies and hypocrisy, both in himself and in relation to others. Therefore he does not want truth to be spoken to him, and avoids speaking it to others; and all of these dispositions, so remote from justice and reason, have a natural root in his heart.

There is an unbridgeable gulf between Fielding's Good Nature and Pascal's *racine naturelle dans son coeur,* and although Fielding despises lying he does not abhor it with the violence of Puritans like Defoe: "It is the concealing of all other crimes; it is the sheep's clothing hung upon the wolf's back, it is the Pharisee's prayer, the whore's blush, the hypocrite's paint, the murderer's smile, the thief's cloak; 'tis Joab's embrace and Judas's kiss; in a word, it is mankind's darling sin and the devil's distinguishing character."

Fearing fallen nature as they did, the Puritans—and severe moralists like Johnson—could sternly denounce error excused by sincerity. Johnson detested *Tom Jones*. Fielding finds himself in a more awkward if also a more genial position, insisting that character is expressed in action but discounting many of the particular actions that characters perform.

> A single bad act no more constitutes a villain in life, than a single bad part on the stage. The passions, like the managers of a playhouse, often force men upon parts, without consulting their judgment, and sometimes without any regard to their talents. Thus the man, as well as the player, may condemn what he himself acts.

In classical ethics morality attaches to choices rather than personality, because only in the act of choice, as Aristotle explains in the *Ethics,* is the moral individual visible. The entire plot of *Tom Jones,* like other fictions in the tradition of the *Odyssey,* is a series of choices, so that it is as Aristotelian in its ethical conception as in its artistic plan. But as a Christian, Fielding could hardly remain at ease with such an ethics. Though he hated Methodism for preferring faith to works, on a deeper level he was committed to the idea of the moral personality as a continuous state of being rather than acting. The Tom who acts is making his moral nature visible to other people, but his good nature precedes all of his actions and remains unblemished by his erroneous ones. For this reason Empson is able to say, surprisingly but persuasively, that Tom's innate goodness resembles the right acting of the Calvinist elect, no doubt because both Calvin and Fielding "had seriously puzzled their heads over the Gospel, and tried to give its paradoxes their full weight." Where Fielding differs from the Calvinists is in the degree to which he is willing to overlook or forgive human fallibility. Again and again Tom does those things which he ought not to have done, and yet there is health in him.

What defines Fielding's distance from Puritan writers most profoundly is his openness to the attractions of desire. "Reason is but choosing," Milton declares in *Areopagitica,* and God the Father concurs in *Paradise Lost:* "Reason also is choice." Like nearly everyone in his time

Fielding affirms that reason should direct passion, but he affirms also that choice is emotional as well as rational. We choose what we long for, and if Allworthy has a fault it is the temperateness of his feelings and his tendency to translate them into rational categories. The embattled Puritan self retreats into its island or inner castle; Fielding's characters commit themselves to the open road, a world full of possibilities for pleasure as well as for action and choice.

In Defoe pleasure is a disease or drug that lulls the conscience asleep: "So possible is it for us to roll ourselves up in wickedness, till we grow invulnerable by conscience; and that sentinel, once dozed, sleeps fast, not to be awakened while the tide of pleasure continues to flow, or till something dark and dreadful brings us to ourselves again." Anything that deranges the reason is, in this tradition, a betrayal of the true self, as Augustine says ruefully of sexual intercourse: "So intense is the pleasure that when it reaches its climax there is an almost total extinction of mental alertness; the intellectual sentries, as it were, are overwhelmed." Fielding, very differently, maintains that physical hunger is inseparable from the highest forms of love. Sex in *Tom Jones* is wonderfully various and not reducible to any single code, however much we are supposed to approve Allworthy's solemn lectures on the subject. Tom is wrong but excusable to sleep with Molly, less wrong to sleep with the mammalian Mrs. Waters, more wrong to sleep with the reptilian Lady Bellaston. In *Clarissa* sex is defiling; in *Tom Jones* it is good in itself though capable, like other good things, of being badly misused (there are glances at sadism in Northerton and Blifil). In Richardson's world you are either defiled or pure. In Fielding's world there are a few great sinners, not many saints, and a wide range of mortals in between.

A similar point can be made about a less inflammatory subject: drunkenness, that abomination in the eyes of Puritans, which Defoe startlingly represents as releasing inadmissible Oedipal impulses.

> That was a good story, whether real or invented, of the devil tempting a young man to murder his father. "No," he said, "that was unnatural." "Why then," says the devil, "Go and lie with your mother." "No," says he, "that is abominable." "Well then," says the devil, "if you will do nothing else to oblige me, go and get drunk." "Ay, ay," says the fellow, "I'll do that"; so he went and made himself drunk as a swine, and when he was drunk, he murdered his father, and lay with his mother.

Alcohol is far less alarming in Fielding's world, where "it was Mr. Western's custom every afternoon, as soon as he was drunk, to hear his daughter play on the harpsichord." *In vino veritas,* but not a Puritan *veritas;* Western drunk is much like Western sober. In Defoe drunkenness produces an abdication of the best self, in Fielding an intensification of it, and we despise Blifil when he exploits the joy with which Tom gets drunk to celebrate Allworthy's recovery from illness.

The point is not just that Fielding was more tolerant than the Puritans, or that he understood love and pleasure while they did not. Milton at least had nothing to learn about the imaginative power of love, with his Eve who tells Adam "With thee conversing I forget all time." What is at stake is Fielding's refusal to see life as an all-or-nothing test, with sex the principal arena in which the individual stands or falls. This in turn implies a radical disagreement with the Puritans about fallen life and about the degree to which one can afford to give in to desire. Allworthy is perhaps absurd when he calls love oxymoronically a "rational passion," especially since he is addressing the wrong audience, earnestly rebuking Jenny Jones for a lapse she has not committed. But in a digression in *Amelia,* his last novel, Fielding himself maintains that the intoxication of desire can be resisted if love is "nicely watched, pruned, and cultivated." This is what the Puritans rejected as impossible. In their terms Fielding has sold out to the love of creatures, and his comic fiction is an abdication of the writer's duty to represent the realities of human life.

MIMESIS AND ARTIFICE

The eighteenth century was committed to mimesis, but the question was whether mimesis should assert or conceal its artificiality. Augustan neoclassicism marks the absolute ending of the Renaissance, during which it had been normal to claim that art and nature both imitate a higher reality. In such a theory there is no question of inferior imitation, for as Lewis says, "Art and nature become rival copies of the same supersensuous original, and there is no reason why art should not sometimes be the better of the two." By the eighteenth century the old harmony between microcosm and macrocosm was fast disappearing, and the Romantic idea of an imaginative heterocosm had not yet arrived. Aesthetic theory now depended on a more literal and less idealizing interpretation of mimesis. Its function was to generalize "philosophically" from the otherwise chaotic data of experience, which in practice tended to mean selection of certain details and omission of others.

But selection, in turn, might seem arbitrary even if obligatory, as Johnson indicates in the *Preface to Shakespeare* with his conflicting claims that Shakespeare mirrors the complexity of real life yet fails to depict life in a morally instructive way. In the year following the publication of *Tom Jones,* Johnson criticized contemporary fiction in terms that reject mere mimesis:

> It is justly considered as the greatest excellency of art to imitate nature, but it is necessary to distinguish those parts of nature which are most proper for imitation; greater care is still re-quired in representing life, which is so often discoloured by passion or deformed by wickedness. If the world be promis-cuously described, I cannot see of what use it can be to read the account, or why it may not be as safe to turn the eye immediately upon mankind as upon a mirror which shows all that presents itself without discrimination.

Yet it is Fielding, after all, who glories in the selecting and shaping power of art, and Johnson who says gruffly at another time, "I had rather see the portrait of a dog that I know, than all the allegorical paintings they can show me in the world." Art must generalize from the actual, not escape into fantasy, for "a story is a picture either of an individual or of human nature in general; if it be false, it is a picture of nothing." Johnson disliked his friend Goldsmith's *Vicar of Wakefield,* with its ironic romance conventions, and told Fanny Burney that "there is nothing of real life in it, and very little of nature. It is a mere fanciful performance."

Fielding, to whom Johnson's position must seem both literalizing and morally heavy-handed, believes as Ehrenpreis says "that art reveals the truth through seeming, while life misleads us through artfulness." His attraction to comedy is therefore more than merely temperamental. Comedy is the genre that celebrates its own art while exposing the artful behavior of our fellow men—the mannerisms and deceptions which, in Horace Walpole's words, "have rendered man a fictitious animal." The genre most congenial to Puritanism was tragedy, which attributes art to the supreme dramatist or at least to the inherent order of things. Since its goal is to represent the inexorable connection of events, a tragedy has every reason to plant clues that will later be shown to reveal structure; *Tom Jones* is far from unique in this regard, and it is no accident that Coleridge praised its plot in the same breath with Sophocles' *Oedipus.*

But as Nietzsche points out, a tragic plot must seem to unwind inevitably, not to be manipulated into place. "Aeschylean-Sophoclean tragedy employed the most ingenious devices in the initial scenes to place in the spectator's hands, as if by chance, all the threads necessary for a complete understanding—a trait proving that noble artistry which, as it were, masks the *necessary* formal element and makes it appear accidental." The comedy of *Tom Jones* does exactly the opposite. Though it does mount an immense structure of relationships among events, many of them remain the effects of pure chance, and the function of the plot is therefore to make accidents seem necessary.

These considerations tend toward the metaphysical implications of Fielding's story, which must be postponed for the moment while we continue to consider the relation between imitation and artifice. That *Tom Jones* is an artifact is made clear throughout. It is a "history"—that is, a narrated story, as in the double meaning of the French *histoire*—"which hath employed some thousands of hours in the composing." Puritan fiction, committed to an illusion of literal veracity, presents itself as first-person memoir or as letters written "to the moment," but history requires a *histor* to shape and interpret its myriad details, whether it is Fielding presenting an imagined tale or Gibbon recounting the fall of Rome. In repeated playful references to the special powers that authors are endowed with, Fielding pays homage to the multiple ironies of Cervantes. When Sancho is amazed that the narrator of his adventures could know about events he never saw, Quixote explains, "I promise you, the author of our history will be some sage enchanter, for to such as they nothing they choose to write about is hidden."

The Puritan *narrator absconditus* has to pretend not to exist at all, ascribing all authority to Almighty God and evading the question of narrative authority. Fielding insists on the specialized role of an author who creates a book, and boasts indeed that he has created a new kind of book with its own "laws." But it is also true that whereas Defoe must pretend to be the real Crusoe, the real Fielding stays distinct from the narrator whom he has "created" to conduct the story.

> As I am, in reality, the founder of a new province of writing, so I am at liberty to make what laws I please therein. And these laws, my readers, whom I consider as my subjects, are bound to believe in and to obey; with which that they may readily and cheerfully comply, I do hereby assure them that I shall principally regard their ease and advantage in all such

institutions: for I do not, like a *jure divino* tyrant, imagine that they are my slaves or my commodity. I am, indeed, set over them for their own good only, and was created for their use, and not they for mine.

The time will come, as Fielding remarks in his affecting "Farewell to the Reader," when he himself must die, but the narrator of *Tom Jones* is a permanent presence, an idealized and specialized projection of the author, whose voice will forever invite new readers to join in compact with him. What that narrator offers is a fictional equivalent of the social contract, in which he and his readers agree upon an artificial construction (the novel, the state) that is designed to afford mutual satisfaction.

In this as in other ways, Fielding is more like Milton than like the authors of the fictions that came later. *Paradise Lost* is the most impersonal of poems but is controlled by a narrator who comments on the action, addresses and warns the characters, and confesses his relation to the blind and isolated John Milton in Restoration London. But that commanding figure, speaking with the inspired voice of a prophet, is always forbidding, and Johnson confessed that we lay *Paradise Lost* down and forget to take it up again—"We read Milton for instruction, retire harassed and overburdened, and look elsewhere for recreation; we desert our master, and seek for companions." Fielding, comparing his tale to stagecoach travel and to festive banqueting, promises to supply that recreation and be that companion.

The narrator of *Tom Jones* is a guide who keeps encouraging the reader to pursue his own way, often supplying misleading hints that get him lost in order to find him again. But this is altogether different from Bunyan's "Wouldest thou lose thyself," because Bunyan proposes a radical opening up of the reader's consciousness, while Fielding invites the reader to join in a game. Like Bunyan, Fielding aspires to teach, but what he teaches is knowledge of the world, not knowledge of the self, much as Locke (that essayistic philosopher) says that the understanding's "searches after truth are a sort of hawking and hunting, wherein the very pursuit makes a great part of the pleasure." Moreover, the hidden clues are all visible on a second reading of the novel, during which the reader is divided into two parts, the hoodwinked victim of the first reading and the enlightened spectator who now knows what really happened. Sometimes these clues take a general form, as in Bridget Allworthy's repeated shows of fondness to young Tom; once we know she is his mother, we realize that the fondness is real and not feigned (as the narrator had tempted us to believe). Sometimes the clues expose turning points where the plot might have taken a different course, for example when the lawyer Dowling very nearly lets slip the information that Tom is Allworthy's nephew, and realizes just in time that Tom doesn't know it—a discovery which, as we later perceive, enables Dowling to blackmail Blifil as the price for keeping the secret. And sometimes the clues uncover unexpected depths, as when Blifil, having just learned who Tom's parents were, insults him by observing that Tom does *not* know it. Here, on second reading, we know what Tom cannot possibly know, and our knowledge allows us to see that Blifil's cruelty is diabolical.

In this way *Tom Jones* becomes a kind of thought experiment that offers a simplified version of the complexity of life, whereas Puritan narrative insists on retaining that complexity in all its mysteriousness. If in Kermode's terms we are all outsiders when we read the old kind of providential narrative, then a fiction like *Tom Jones* allows us to be outsiders and insiders simultaneously. What holds it together is the narrator's ability to make us believe that he is experienced and wise. He is no mere device for getting the story told, but the essential medium through which it makes sense, so that the essayistic element in this kind of novel is its absolute sine qua non. And in this Fielding is deeply traditional, just as the Puritan fiction of nonfictional veracity is modern, for as Benjamin says, "Counsel woven into the fabric of real life is wisdom. The art of storytelling is reaching its end because the epic side of truth, wisdom, is dying out."

Since the narrator rejoices in his role instead of concealing it, he is at liberty to declare which facts shall count as significant instead of accumulating them without apparent art in the expectation that they will interpret themselves. In Puritan narrative, details have a twofold function. First, they are clues that need to be carefully scanned in a universe where everything may carry significance, since it is God who has planted the clues to his hidden plot. We can never be certain which bits of data will turn out to be essential. And second, they provide the necessary illusion of reality, since so much depends on persuading the reader that the story is not merely *like* life but in an absolute sense (even if allegorical) is *identical with* life. Whether by instinct or design, Defoe superbly captures the indecision of a man fussing over minute details: "By and by I saw a great fowl like a hawk sit upon a tree within shot; so to let Friday understand a little what I would do, I called him to me again, pointed at the fowl which was indeed a parrot, though I thought it had been a hawk, I say pointing to the parrot." Having no use for this kind of verisimilitude, Fielding enjoys making fun of it: "He accordingly ate either a rabbit or a fowl, I never could with any tolerable certainty discover which."

The Man of the Hill in *Tom Jones* is a kind of parodic Crusoe, with his animal-skin clothes and retreat from the life of his fellow men. And the story he tells, with its youthful crimes and later disgust with human nature, is a version of the Puritan first-person narrative, imprisoned within the narrowness of an obsessive point of view. Formal realism is thus embedded, by way of counter-example, in the middle of Fielding's comic epic, and proves (of course) no match for Fielding's medley of literary devices in presenting an image of truth. The old man himself is lamentably feeble at drawing conclusions from his own experience. When he generalizes about others he is merely reductive—"In France a knave is dressed like a fop, and in the northern countries like a sloven. But human nature is everywhere the same, everywhere the object of detestation and scorn"—and when he is faced with an actual chance to help another person he remains unmoved while Tom rushes to the aid of a woman in distress. Imprisoned within a dreadful privacy, the old man badly needs a comic narrator to tell his story for him and to liberate him into the complexities of social existence. The other first-person story-teller in *Tom Jones,* Harriet Fitzpatrick, is (like Moll Flanders) one of those persons whom experience has taught to be cunning rather than good, and both ethically and aesthetically she is an unreliable narrator. But her life rapidly gets absorbed in the great body of the host organism, *Tom Jones,* and far from continuing to be the heroine of her own story, she is compelled to take her place as a minor character in Fielding's. It is worth noting that selective omission of embarrassing facts is common even to the best characters; both Tom and Sophia do it.

The ambiguous relationship between art and life is superbly imagined in the episode in which Partridge goes with Tom to see *Hamlet,* and naively praises the crude Claudius while dismissing Garrick's Hamlet as unremarkable. "'He the best player!' cries Partridge with a contemptuous sneer, 'why I could act as well as he myself. I am sure if I had seen a ghost, I should have looked in the very same manner, and done just as he did.'" Jones has looked forward to seeing in Partridge "the simple dictates of nature, unimproved indeed, but likewise unadulterated by art," and that is exactly what he gets. Partridge does his best to remember that "it is only a play," but unlike the bombastic performances he has seen in the country, this one is so brilliantly acted that he keeps forgetting its artifice (especially when it touches on his personal obsession, ghosts). His reaction *is* natural, and is the highest possible tribute to Garrick, whose acting is so accomplished that it doesn't look like acting.

Life, like art, has its consummate actors. The very next chapter in *Tom Jones* is devoted to that expert hypocrite Blifil, whose acting is mistaken for nature by nearly everyone. But that does not mean that acting is always wicked, only that we have to learn to interpret an actor's motives. The same principle holds true for any artificial form, which is to say for any human pursuit ("Art is man's nature," Burke memorably said). What Barthes describes in professional wrestling is just as true of *Tom Jones:*

> What the public wants is the image of passion, not passion itself. There is no more a problem of truth in wrestling than in the theatre. In both, what is expected is the intelligible representation of moral situations which are usually private. This emptying out of interiority to the benefit of its exterior signs, this exhaustion of the content by the form, is the very principle of triumphant classical art.

To put it less provocatively, content may well be significant but is impotent without form, while form can be effective even if the content it conveys is wholly artificial (Garrick has not seen a ghost and is only simulating fear). We know that Fielding was fascinated throughout his life with the puppet theatre, which also appears in *Tom Jones,* and liked to insist that life itself was like a puppet show. In fiction as in life, one develops a critical intelligence that can see behind the performance and judge it.

For all of its headlong concatenation of events, *Tom Jones* is offered to the reader as a running commentary on human life, with moments of dialogue and memorable scenes held in suspension like tableaux. Yet the impression persists that these moments are selected by the narrator from a stable reality larger than himself, rather than being generated arbitrarily for the purpose of giving amusement and instruction. Whereas Puritans tended to see life emblematically as a collection of nodal points that emerge from the flux of time, Fielding sees life as a structure of causality that has to be appreciated as a whole, which may not be possible in actual experience, but can be achieved in imagination on a second reading of his novel. Kermode has said that the epistolary method allows Richardson to merge *chronos* with *kairos,* extracting supreme significance from particular events; Fielding insists on a *chronos* that embodies meaning in its totality, rather than yielding up meaning by a breakthrough into *kairos*. The Puritan novel need not construct a coherent chronology, since it is enough to suggest the stream of experience within which (as in Augustine's *Confessions*) man lives in psychological time, seeking to identify the crucial moments among the welter of unassimilable details. So *Tom Jones* has its famously perfect plot while *Robinson Crusoe* has, in that sense, almost no plot at all. Puritan poetics requires an excess of detail as the background from which significant detail can emerge epiphanically; Fielding's poetics finds significance in the whole, and is committed to showing how everything is interconnected. This narrative epistemology is reflected in the world of social relationships. The solitary Puritan pilgrim leaves his earthly home forever, avoids unnecessary entanglements with "creatures," and arrives at last at the promised land. The gregarious traveler in Fielding gets valuable assistance from the people he meets on the road, redefines his rightful place in the social order, and ends up where he began (in Tom's case, reunited with Allworthy of Paradise Hall).

These considerations suggest how different Fielding is from Puritan writers when he uses emblematic imagery. Emblems are planted and then revealed by the narrator as a way of making particular points, not embedded in a reality which is itself emblematic by a God who teaches man to interpret emblems. This is strikingly apparent at the very end of the book, when Tom swears eternal fidelity to Sophia by making her look at her own reflection in a mirror.

> "There, behold it there, in that lovely figure, in that face, that shape, those eyes, that mind which shines through those eyes: can the man who shall be in possession of these be inconstant?" . . . Sophia blushed, and half smiled; but forcing again her brow into a frown, "If I am to judge," said she, "of the future by the past, my image will no more remain in your heart when I am out of your sight, than it will in this glass when I am out of the room." "By heaven, by all that is sacred," said Jones, "it never was out of my heart."

Undoubtedly Fielding turns Sophia's reflected image into a kind of emblem, but this is closer to a conceit than to an intuition of celestial truth, and it can hardly be right to conclude that Sophia's "true identity is ideal, an abstraction." The name Sophia means "wisdom," but Sophia Western is not wisdom personified as Spenser's Una is truth personified. She is a flesh-and-blood young woman, up whose skirts admiring innkeepers have peered, and Tom wins her because he is learning to be wise, under her encouraging influence of course, not because she herself is wisdom. The emblem is only an emblem, an arbitrary sign whose meaning derives from the richer reality of the living Sophia Western, and she in turn derives from the reality of women like Fielding's dead wife, whom the fiction brings back to life even as it concedes that Fielding himself will soon join her in the grave.

> Come, bright Love of Fame, inspire my glowing breast. . . . Foretell me that some tender maid, whose grandmother is yet unborn, hereafter, when, under the fictitious name of Sophia, she reads the real worth which once existed in my Charlotte, shall from her sympathetic breast, send forth the heaving sigh. . . . Comfort me by a solemn assurance, that when the little parlour in which I sit at this instant, shall be reduced to a worse furnished box, I shall be read, with honour, by those who never knew nor saw me, and whom I shall neither know nor see.

It is not the narrator but Tom who allegorizes Sophia's image in the glass, pointing out her reflection as a way of guaranteeing his fidelity. He is showing her a visual earnest of their relationship, not stepping outside the narrative as Bunyan might to make a metaphysical point.

Even a Platonist would hold that the good cannot be loved abstractly, but is known in embodied form, and Tom's love for the real Sophia is essential for learning—what might seem alien to his ebullient "good nature"—the virtues of prudence and temperance. But Platonism is closer to the Augustinian tradition than to Fielding's worldly cheerfulness, for as Tuve says of Spenser, "We realize that vast influence of Augustine's discussion of temperance as rightly directed love. Guyon does not have to learn how to have just enough love of the world, a reasonable amount of lust. He is to love good *instead*." No author is less likely than Fielding to denounce, as the Puritans did, the "love of creatures." A recurrent (and suggestive) emblem in *Tom Jones* is Sophia's muff, which Jones handles and kisses passionately, and which serves as the physical correlative for sexual desire when Sophia is briefly tempted to martyr herself to her father's commands. "Sophia was charmed with the contemplation of so heroic an action, and began to compliment herself with much premature flattery, when Cupid, who lay hid in her muff, suddenly crept out." One should not forget that immediately after Tom shows Sophia her image in the glass, her father, reconciled to Tom by reason of his unexpected good fortune, bursts in exclaiming "To her boy, to her, go to her.—That's it, little honeys, O that's it!" When Tom politely beseeches him to not overwhelm Sophia's modesty, he retorts decisively, "Beseech mine arse."

While appreciating Western's sheer comic energy one ought not to overlook his meanness and cruelty, and it is an exaggeration (though a pardonable one) to call him the Atlas "on whose broad and presumably hairy back everything else rests." Still it is true that Fielding's world has room in it for the Dionysian Western as well as the Apollonian Allworthy, and more than once Western manages to express what subtler characters miss, the fact that all normal human beings do indeed want the same things. (It is odd, though, that Western himself exhibits no active sexual interest. Presumably this is because Fielding is afraid he will seem a lecherous old man if he pursues women—though Hugh Griffith, in his immortal impersonation of Western in Tony Richardson's film, manages to include lechery among his tendencies.) No impassable gulf is fixed between Tom's "by all that is sacred" and Western's "beseech mine arse." In *Clarissa* different styles of speech reflect incommensurable versions of reality; just the opposite is true in *Tom Jones,* where no misunderstanding is ever permanent.

As always, we have to recognize that "realism" is too general a term to be used as an abstraction, and indeed is more aptly used in its adjectival form. A given work may seem "realistic" to its readers—not necessarily to later readers—but it does not contain or possess an entity called "realism." In many of the familiar senses of the term, Defoe and Richardson are far more realistic than Fielding. Yet it is also true that Fielding exhibits, as they do not, what J. P. Stern admires in Dickens, signs of "the *eros* that binds him to this world." For all of their mimetic detail, Defoe's novels reflect a withdrawal into the self rather than a commitment to social reality. *Tom Jones,* committed so enthusiastically to social reality, pays homage to *Don Quixote* as the great model for fictions in which reality tests and explodes every form of solipsism. The process is powerful because it forces us to admit, just as Swift's Houyhnhnms do, the unworkability of our highest ideals in the world we live in, and as Stern says the results can be painful: "The life of Don Quixote is a challenge (among the most poignant in all literature) to our customary notions of reality, but the challenge is rebutted at every point."

In his study of quixotic fictions Alexander Welsh stresses the centrality of the problem of justice, which can never resolve itself into the absolute structure that the heart longs for, and forever thwarts the quixotic effort to attain it. But the impossibility of justice does not prevent us from wanting it, and quixotic action tends to accomplish more than official inaction. "The tradition of the knight errant as justicer, therefore, is not as silly as it seems; or rather it is silly, as quixotic fictions demonstrate, but there is no alternative institution." Fielding the lawyer had no illusions about the law, and Abraham Adams in *Joseph Andrews* is very much a quixotic seeker of justice. Yet in the end Fielding endorses the *nomos* far more decisively than Cervantes does, tending to imply that injustice is the result of particular abuses rather than of a disturbance at the heart of things. Adams's naiveté is at once an unworldly folly which we cannot afford to imitate and a saintly criticism of the world that persecutes him, but even at his most quixotic he is more like an abnormally well-read baby than like a Cervantean visionary. "He was besides a man of good sense, good parts, and good nature; but was at the same time as entirely ignorant of the ways of this world, as an infant just entered into it could possibly be." In Welsh's scheme fiction develops toward an increasing recognition of the universe itself as a cruel practical joke, in the spirit of Ortega's remark, "Surrounding culture . . . lies the barbarous, brutal, mute, meaningless reality of things." Fielding, very differently, wants to come to terms with the shape of reality and with the human relationships that society ought to confirm. It is notable that in *Tom Jones* he presents a Sancho (Partridge) but no Quixote. Tom both deals out justice effectively, for instance when he thrashes the brutal Northerton, and receives it abundantly, when Blifil is exposed and Tom is restored to union with Allworthy and Sophia.

The deepest affinity of *Tom Jones* with the Quixote tradition lies elsewhere: not in putting the concept of justice into question, but in holding imaginative constructs of reality up to inspection even while endorsing, in the end, the notion of a stable and coherent universe. The Puritan novel tests the individual, but only indirectly and covertly does it ever test the universe that does the testing. Hence, as we have seen in both *Crusoe* and *Clarissa,* a heavy freight of fantasy can be passed off as mimetic veracity, since the very existence of fiction is never acknowledged. Clarissa sees herself as a tragic heroine because she *is* a tragic heroine; Lovelace is wrong to see himself as a comic hero, because life is not a comedy. Fielding's kind of novel, on the other hand, affirms the order of things even while exposing the incompleteness and private distortion of individual perceptions of it. The narrator stands behind the story to guarantee its integrity, both by admitting that he has made it up—what no narrator in Defoe or Richardson could possibly admit—

and also by affirming that what he mas made up corresponds to the larger coherence of things.

In his dual emphasis on romance (in story) and irony (in presentation), Fielding exposes the fantasy of naive realism and frankly acknowledges his own fantasy. As Marthe Robert says, the realistic novel rejects romance as insincere fantasizing, hence denying its own romantic elements, while the opposed kind of novel openly acknowledges that it is only "a set of figures and forms" while insisting that reality cannot be expressed without them. In Fielding romance works to expose but also to reward the quixotic basis of every human imagination, so that the ironic *Tom Jones* is at the same time a superb feat of wish-fulfillment.

Chronology

1707	Born at Sharpham Park, Glastonbury, Somerset.
1719–24	Studies at Eton.
1728	His first published work—*The Masquerade,* a satiric poem; his first produced play—*Love in Several Masques.*
1728–29	Studies letters at the University of Leyden until August 1729, when he returns to London.
1730–37	Dramatist—e.g., *The Author's Farce, Tom Thumb, The Tragedy of Tragedies, The Grub-Street Opera, The Modern Husband, The Miser, Don Quixote in England, Pasquin, Eurydice,* and *The Historical Register.* All his plays are comedies.
1734	Elopes with Charlotte Cradock.
1737	The Licensing Act cuts short his career as playwright; studies law at the Middle Temple (London).
1739–41	Edits *The Champion.*
1740	Called to the Bar at the Middle Temple. Richardson's *Pamela* published.
1741	Publishes *Shamela.*
1742	Publishes *Joseph Andrews.*
1743	*Miscellanies* (essays, poems, *Jonathan Wild,* and *A Journey from this World to the Next*).
1744	Charlotte Cradock Fielding dies.
1745	Writes pamphlets for the Hanoverian cause against the Jacobites—*A Serious Address to the People of Great Britain, The History of the Present Rebellion,* and *A Dialogue between the Devil, the Pope, and the Pretender.*
1745–46	Edits *The True Patriot.*
1747	Marries Mary Daniel. Edits *The Jacobite's Journal* (Hanoverian propaganda).

1748   Supplements his income by running a puppet theater under the name of Madame de la Nash. Writes Richardson a letter of praise for *Clarissa*. Commissioned as magistrate for Westminster (London).

1749   Founds the Universal Register Office. Commissioned as magistrate for the County of Middlesex. Publishes *Tom Jones*, *A Charge to the Grand Jury*, and *The Case of Bosavern Penlez*.

1751   Publishes *Enquiry into the Causes of the Late Increase of Robbers* and *Amelia*.

1752   Edits *The Covent-Garden Journal*.

1753   Publishes *Proposal for Making an Effectual Provision for the Poor*. Carries out plan for ridding London of gangs of robbers, laying foundations for modern police force and for Scotland Yard.

1754   Revises *Jonathan Wild*. Resigns from magistracy due to gout, jaundice, dropsy, and asthma. Travels to Lisbon and writes *Voyage to Lisbon* (published posthumously in 1755). Dies and is buried in Lisbon.

Contributors

HAROLD BLOOM, Sterling Professor of the Humanities at Yale University, is the author of *The Anxiety of Influence, Poetry and Repression,* and many other volumes of literary criticism. His forthcoming study, *Freud: Transference and Authority,* attempts a full-scale reading of all of Freud's major writings. A MacArthur Prize Fellow, he is general editor of five series of literary criticism published by Chelsea House. During 1987–88, he was appointed Charles Eliot Norton Professor of Poetry at Harvard University.

IAN WATT, Professor of English at Stanford University, has taught both in England and the United States, specializing in eighteenth-century literature and Joseph Conrad. *The Rise of the Novel: Studies in Defoe, Richardson, and Fielding* is only one among the many books he has written and edited.

WAYNE C. BOOTH is Distinguished Service Professor of English at the University of Chicago. *The Rhetoric of Fiction, The Rhetoric of Irony, Modern Dogma and the Rhetoric of Assent* are among the works that have come out of his interest in rhetoric and eighteenth-century literature.

MARTIN PRICE is Sterling Professor of English at Yale University. He is the author of *Swift's Rhetorical Art, To the Palace of Wisdom: Studies in Order and Energy from Dryden to Blake,* and *Forms of Life.*

RONALD PAULSON, Professor of English at The Johns Hopkins University, specializes in seventeenth- and eighteenth-century literature and painting. He has written on Hogarth, Rowlandson, Turner, and Constable, as well as on Swift, Fielding, and others.

MARTIN C. BATTESTIN is the William R. Kenan, Jr., Professor of English at the University of Virginia. He is the author of *The Providence of Wit:*

Aspects of Form in Augustan Literature and the Arts and *The Moral Basis of Henry Fielding's Art,* as well as the editor of the Clarendon and Wesleyan editions of *Tom Jones, Amelia,* and *Joseph Andrews.*

GRETE EK teaches English at the University of Oslo.

MANUEL SCHONHORN is Professor of English at Southern Illinois University, where he specializes in eighteenth-century history of ideas, Defoe, Pope, and Fielding.

LEOPOLD DAMROSCH, JR., is Professor of English at the University of Maryland. He is the author of *Samuel Johnson and the Tragic Sense, The Uses of Johnson's Criticism,* and *Symbol and Truth in Blake's Myth.*

Bibliography

Alter, Robert. *Fielding and the Nature of the Novel*. Cambridge: Harvard University Press, 1968.

Anderson, Howard. "Answers to the Author of *Clarissa*: Theme and Narrative Technique in *Tom Jones* and *Tristram Shandy*." *Philological Quarterly* 51 (1972): 859–73.

Baker, Sheridan. "Bridget Allworthy: The Creative Pressures of Fielding's Plot." *Papers of the Michigan Academy of Science, Arts, and Letters* 52 (1967): 345–56.

————. "Fielding and the Irony of Form." *Eighteenth-Century Studies* 2, (1968): 138–54.

Battestin, Martin C. "Fielding's Definition of Wisdom: Some Functions of Ambiguity and Emblem in *Tom Jones*." *ELH* 35 (1968): 188–217.

————, ed. *Twentieth Century Interpretations of* Tom Jones. Englewood Cliffs, N.J.: Prentice-Hall, 1968.

Bell, Michael. "A Note on Drama and the Novel: Fielding's Contribution." *Novel* 3 (1970): 119–28.

Booth, Wayne. *The Rhetoric of Fiction*. Chicago: University of Chicago Press, 1961.

Brown, Laura S. "Drama and Novel in Eighteenth-Century England." *Genre* 13 (1980): 287–304.

Burke, John J., Jr. "History without History: Henry Fielding's Theory of Fiction." In *A Provision of Human Nature: Essays on Fielding and Others in Honor of Miriam Austin Locke,* edited by Donald Kay, 45–63. University: University of Alabama Press, 1977.

Champion, Larry S., ed. *Quick Springs of Sense: Studies in the Eighteenth Century.* Athens: University of Georgia Press, 1974.

Crane, R. S. "The Plot of *Tom Jones*." *Journal of General Education* 4 (1950): 112–30.

Digeon, Aurelien. *The Novels of Fielding*. London: Routledge & Sons, 1925.

Ehrenpreis, Irvin. *Fielding*: Tom Jones. London: E. Arnold, 1964.

Empson, William. "Tom Jones." *The Kenyon Review* 20, (1958): 217–49.

Folkenflik, Robert, ed. *The English Hero 1660–1800*. Newark: University of Delaware Press, 1982.

Golden, Morris. *Fielding's Moral Psychology*. Amherst: University of Massachusetts Press, 1966.

Goldknopf, David. "The Failure of Plot in *Tom Jones*." *Criticism* 11 (1969): 262–74.

Harrison, Bernard. *Henry Fielding's* Tom Jones: *The Novelist as Moral Philosopher.* London: Sussex University Press, 1975.

Hilson, J. C., M. M. B. Jones, and J. R. Watson, eds. *Augustan Worlds*. New York: Barnes & Noble, 1978.

Hunter, J. Paul. *Occasional Form: Henry Fielding and the Chains of Circumstance*. Baltimore and London: The Johns Hopkins University Press, 1975.

Hutchens, Eleanor Newman. *Irony in* Tom Jones. University: University of Alabama Press, 1965.

Iser, Wolfgang. *The Implied Reader: Patterns of Communication in Prose Fiction from Bunyan to Beckett*. Baltimore and London: The Johns Hopkins University Press, 1974.

Karl, Frederick R. *The Adversary Literature: The English Novel in the Eighteenth Century. A Study in Genre*. New York: Farrar, Straus & Giroux, 1974.

Kay, Donald, ed. *A Provision of Human Nature: Essays on Fielding and Others in Honor of Miriam Austin Locke*. University: University of Alabama Press, 1977.

Kermode, Frank. "Richardson and Fielding." *Cambridge Journal* 4 (1950): 106–14.

Kettle, Arnold. *An Introduction to the English Novel*, vol. 1. London: Hutchinson's University Library, 1951.

Lutwack, Leonard. "Mixed and Uniform Prose Styles in the Novel." *The Journal of Aesthetics and Art Criticism* 18, no. 3 (1960): 350–57.

Mack, Maynard and Ian Gregor, eds. *Imagined Worlds: Essays on Some English Novels and Novelists in Honour of John Butt*. London: Methuen, 1968.

Mandel, Jerome. "The Man of the Hill and Mrs. Fitzpatrick: Character and Narrative Technique in *Tom Jones*." *Papers on Language and Literature* 5 (1969): 26–38.

Miller, Henry Knight. "The 'Digressive' Tales in Fielding's *Tom Jones* and the Perspective of Romance." *Philological Quarterly* 54 (1975): 258–74.

———. *Henry Fielding's* Tom Jones *and the Romance Tradition*. Victoria, B.C.: English Literary Studies, 1976.

Miller, Henry Knight, Eric Rothstein, and G. S. Rousseau, eds. *The Augustan Milieu: Essays Presented to Louis A. Landa*. Oxford: Clarendon Press, 1970.

Murry, John Middleton. *Unprofessional Essays*. London: Jonathan Cape, 1956.

Paulson, Ronald. *Satire and the Novel in Eighteenth-Century England*. New Haven and London: Yale University Press, 1967.

Preston, John. *The Created Self: The Reader's Role in Eighteenth-Century Fiction*. London: Heinemann, 1970.

Price, Martin. *To the Palace of Wisdom: Studies in Order and Energy from Dryden to Blake*. Carbondale: Southern Illinois University Press, 1964.

Rawson, C. J. "Nature's Dance of Death, Part I: Urbanity and Strain in Fielding, Swift, and Pope." *Eighteenth-Century Studies* 3 (1970): 307–38.

Ribble, Frederick G. "Aristotle and the 'Prudence' Theme of *Tom Jones*." *Eighteenth-Century Studies* 15 (1981): 26–47.

Rogers, Pat. *Fielding: A Biography*. London: Elek, 1979.

Sacks, Sheldon. *Fiction and the Shape of Belief: A Study of Henry Fielding With Glances at Swift, Johnson, and Richardson*. Berkeley and Los Angeles: University of California Press, 1966.

Schonhorn, Manuel. "Fielding's Digressive-Parodic Artistry: *Tom Jones* and The Man of the Hill." *Texas Studies in Literature and Language* 10 (1968): 207–14.

Stevick, Philip. "On Fielding Talking." *College Literature* 1 (1974): 19–33.

Vopat, James B. "Narrative Technique in *Tom Jones*: The Balance of Art and Nature." *The Journal of Narrative Technique* 4 (1974): 144–54.

Watt, Ian. *The Rise of the Novel*. Berkeley and Los Angeles: University of California Press, 1960.

Acknowledgments

"Fielding as Novelist: *Tom Jones*" by Ian Watt from *The Rise of the Novel* by Ian Watt, © 1957 by Ian Watt. Reprinted by permission of the University of California Press.

"'Fielding' in *Tom Jones*" by Wayne C. Booth from *The Rhetoric of Fiction* by Wayne C. Booth, © 1961, 1983 by the University of Chicago. Reprinted by permission of the University of Chicago Press.

"The Subversion of Forms" by Martin Price from *To the Palace of Wisdom: Studies in Order and Energy from Dryden to Blake* by Martin Price, © 1964 by Martin Price. Reprinted by permission.

"Fielding the Novelist: The Lucianic Satirist" by Ronald Paulson from *Satire and the Novel in Eighteenth-Century England* by Ronald Paulson, © 1967 by Yale University. Reprinted by permission of Yale University Press.

"*Tom Jones*: The Argument of Design" (originally entitled "*Tom Jones*: The Argument of Design—Fortune and Providence") by Martin Battestin from *The Augustan Milieu: Essays Presented to Louis A. Landa,* edited by Henry Knight Miller, Eric Rothstein, and G. S. Rousseau, © 1970 by Oxford University Press. Reprinted by permission.

"Glory, Jest, and Riddle: The Masque of Tom Jones in London" by Grete Ek from *English Studies* 60, no. 2 (April 1979), © 1979 by Swets & Zeitlinger, B.V. Reprinted by permission.

"Fielding's Ecphrastic Moment: Tom Jones and His Egyptian Majesty" by Manuel Schonhorn from *Studies in Philology* 78, no. 3 (Summer 1981), © 1981 by Manuel Schonhorn. Reprinted by permission of the author and the University of North Carolina Press.

"*Tom Jones* and the Farewell to Providential Fiction" by Leopold Damrosch, Jr. from *God's Plot and Man's Stories: Studies in the Fictional Imagination from Milton to Fielding* by Leopold Damrosch, Jr., © 1985 by the University of Chicago. Reprinted by permission of the University of Chicago Press.

Index

Adams, Parson (*Joseph Andrews*), character of, 52, 53, 57
Aeneid (Virgil), ecphrasis in, 92–93
Alchemist, The (Jonson), *Tom Jones* compared to, 16, 61
Allworthy, Bridget, character of, 58–59, 115–16
Allworthy, Squire, character of, 47, 105–6
Amelia (Fielding): characterization in, 49; ironic tragedy in, 48–49; ironic treatment of traditional literary forms in, 40; masquerade in, 85; Providence in, 71–72; role of sex in, 26–27, 112; social conservatism in, 17
Amis, Kingsley: Fielding compared to, 40–41; on Fielding, 40
Andrews, Joseph (*Joseph Andrews*), Tom Jones compared to, 56
Apology for the Life of Mr. Colley Cibber, Comedian (Cibber), Fielding on, 42–43
Aristotle: on character development, 18; and Providence, 63; view of human nature of, 20–21

Bellaston, Lady: character of, 81, 82–83, 85; "enslavement" of Tom Jones by, 77, 81, 82–83, 84; relationship to Tom Jones of, 76, 77, 79–81, 82–85; Tom Jones's rejection of, 83
Birth and social station, significance in *Tom Jones* of, 16–17
Blifil, William: character of, 9–10, 28, 116, 118; courtship of Sophia Western of, 9–10
Booby, Lady (*Joseph Andrews*), character of, 57
Bunyan, John, Fielding compared to, 115

Causation: Fielding's view of, 118–19; Puritan view of, 118–19; Richardson's view of, 118
Clarissa Harlowe (Richardson): characterization in, 12–15, 17, 18; *Tom Jones* compared to, 9, 12, 14–15, 17–18, 21, 22, 27, 32; contemporary rivalry with *Tom Jones* of, 2; narrative structure of, 121; plot structure of, 22; Samuel Johnson on moral teachings of, 26; significance of individualism in, 17; use of realism in, 13–14
Character, priority of plot over in *Tom Jones*, 17–18, 22, 24–25
Character development, Aristotle on, 18